I'M COM

I'M COMING OUT

31-Days of Renewal

LISA L. JOHNSON

Copyright © 2021 by Lisa L. Johnson

All rights reserved. This book or parts thereof may not be reproduced, stored in a retrieval system, or transmitted in any form or by any means–electronic, mechanical, photocopy, recording, scanning, or otherwise–except for brief quotations in critical reviews or articles, without the prior written permission of the publisher.

Cover design by Cassy's Touch Publishing, LLC

Published in West Palm Beach, Florida by Cassy's Touch Publishing, LLC. Cassy's Touch Publishing, LLC books, journals, etc., may be ordered through bookseller or by contacting:

www.cassystouch.com

The publisher is not responsible for website (or their content) that are not owned by the publisher.

Scripture taken from the New King James Version®. Copyright © 1982 by Thomas Nelson. Used by permission. All rights reserved.

Visit the author's website at www.lljohnsondivine.com

ISBN: 978-1-7359222-3-2 (hardcover)

ISBN: 978-1-7359222-4-9 (ebook)

Library of Congress Control Number: 2020925800

Printed in the United States of America

Dedication

I dedicate *I'm Coming Out: 31 Days of Renewal* to my children, Rashad, Destinee, and Daniel.

I know that you have experienced similar struggles that I have overcome. While generational cycles are prevalent in our bloodline, the blood of Jesus is powerful to demolish all strongholds and cycles. What God has done for me was through the daily renewing of my mind. When you were young children, I was intentional to survive and thrive because of you. Despite my hurts, disappointments, and even failures, you have witnessed God's grace, mercy, favor, and faithfulness towards me. God has also proven himself faithful to you.

I know that God is already working in and through each of you. I encourage you to walk according to the spirit and not of the flesh, through the renewing of your minds, and you will experience God's best He has for you!

I love each of you with my whole heart!

CONTENTS

	Acknowledgments	ix
	Foreword	xi
	Introduction	xiii
1	Keep The Faith	15
2	Jesus Saves	23
3	That Is Not My Name	29
4	Take Control Of Your Mental Health	37
5	The Power To Succeed	43
6	Am I Living Or Existing?	49
7	Get Off The Merry-Go-Round	57
8	God Is Still In Control	63
9	I Need Help	69
10	The Joy Of The Lord	75
11	Broken	81
12	Be Still	87
13	More Than Enough	93
14	Excluded	99
15	I Need An Understanding	105
16	Are You Fully Protected?	111
17	It's Me I See	117
18	What Are Your Vital Signs?	123
19	Follow The Light	129
20	This Is The Day	135
21	I Hear The Sound	141
22	It's Not About Me	147
23	It Is Good To Praise	153

24	Why Not You?	159
25	I Finally Said Yes	163
26	Walk By Faith	169
27	Telephone Disconnected?	175
28	Jesus Take The Wheel	181
29	Reset	187
30	Renew Your Mind	193
31	Free	199
	Daily Journals	*205*
	Scriptural Reflection	*239*
	Bibliography	*245*

ACKNOWLEDGMENTS

I give God my Father all praise, honor, and glory for allowing me to accomplish my goal of publishing my first book. He has given me the strength to overcome many obstacles and turn them into triumphs. Because of Him, I am here today. Because of God, I am no longer a victim but a victor!

Thank you to my Mom, Dr. Olivia Jones Mack, for introducing me to Jesus Christ at an early age. Thank you for teaching me biblical principles and truths. Thank you for teaching me the power of prayer and for your continuous prayers. Thank you to my three children, Rashad, Destinee, and Daniel, who have witnessed my struggles but, most importantly, my steadfast love toward them and God. Thank you for believing in me and the morals, values, and biblical principles I have instilled in you.

To Cassandra V. Fulwood, Senior Pastor, Oasis Church International, West Palm Beach, Florida; my best friend, confidant, and mentor of thirty years. Words alone cannot express the gratitude I have for everything you have done for me. Thank you for your unconditional love, tireless prayers, and late-night talks when I needed to share my feelings. You have always listened to me and given me sound advice. Thank you for your leadership and guidance in so many areas of my life. Thank you for believing in me and being there with me through thick and thin. Thank you for making this book possible. You have been my true inspiration.

FOREWORD

With all the happenings in our world today, having a source of inspiration and renewal is invaluable. You are in for a treat as you turn each page of *I'm Coming Out: 31 Days of Renewal*. It is a smorgasbord of encouragement where you are sure to glean nuggets that will uplift your spirit.

Not only is this a book of short stories, it is a resource that allows you to engage on a deeper level. At the end of each day, you're given the opportunity to look inward and make resolutions by answering thought-provoking questions. Then at the very end of the book you'll be allowed to freestyle by journaling your aha moments and insights.

Being a warm, open-hearted woman, Lisa L. Johnson provides 31 Days of Renewal and Scriptural Reflection. Practicality and God's Word. What wisdom! Hebrews 4:12 says, *For the word of God is alive and active. Sharper than any double-edged sword, it penetrates even to dividing soul and spirit, joints and marrow; it judges the thoughts and attitudes of the heart.*

I regard *I'm Coming Out: 31 Days of Renewal* as a highly important resource today. In it Lisa L. Johnson opens her heart and creativity with the purpose of sharing hope. Enjoy!

Cassandra V. Fulwood
West Palm Beach, Florida

INTRODUCTION

I'm Coming Out: 31 Days of Renewal was birthed from writing weekly devotionals for my church's prayer page on Facebook. One day I heard God's voice through Holy Spirit say that these devotionals will comprise my first book. Each week I consulted God on what to write. I wanted to ensure that my writing would be impactful and life-changing.

God uses our past, trials, tests, mistakes, and poor decisions and turns them around for our good and His glory. *I'm Coming Out: 31 Days of Renewal* will capture your thoughts as you read about fictional characters and real-life examples of what we encounter as ordinary people who need a Savior and Holy Spirit to lead and guide us through life's journey. This book encourages you to reflect on what you have read and how you can relate to the thoughts within it and renew your mind daily. It will also enable you to impact others around you.

At the end of the 31 days, my prayer is that you will be completely renewed and ready to fulfill your divine destiny and calling, allowing nothing to hinder you.

DAY 1

Keep The Faith

Karen heads off to work, turns on the radio in her vehicle only to hear the news of active Coronavirus "COVID-19" cases in her city. She says aloud to herself, "you've got to be kidding me!" She had just started her new job as a Dental Assistant. Her father passed away a few years ago after being married to her mom (a Christian) for 55 years. Karen and the rest of her family all live in different states. She is a single mom, recently divorced due to infidelity, with two children, ages 5 and 8. Karen has two siblings, who are not as close as before everyone moved away from each other.

A week later, Karen went to work at a local dentist's office. The office manager scheduled a staff meeting and informed them that the office was closing immediately due to the "social distancing" laws and the business's intimate nature for both patients' and employees' health and safety. The office manager informed Karen that the time off from work will be unpaid. That afternoon, the local news reported that all schools in the county would close temporarily. The next day, Karen received a phone call from her aunt that her mother was in ICU at a hospital in New York and tested positive for COVID-19. Karen could not visit her mother due to the travel ban to New York, where the virus was quickly spreading.

Karen, who has experience with God, as never leaving or forsaking her, immediately recalled Psalm 46:1 — *God is our refuge, a very present help in time of trouble.* She began to weep. However, being a woman of faith, she said the following prayer: "Dear God, thank you for being the Creator of both heaven and the earth. Thank you for seeing fit to allow me and my children to be alive and well. Thank you for sitting high and looking low, seeing all of the chaos going on, but you continue making ways out of no ways for your people. Thank you for being a promise-keeper. Thank You, God, for the dentists, co-workers, supervisor, and everyone who has lost employment due to the Coronavirus outbreak and pandemic. God, thank you for my family. Now, my God, ABBA Father, Jehovah Rapha, the God that heals, I ask that you heal my mother's body. I ask that you let your breath be the air that she breathes. Give her strength in her body. Allow the doctors to be confounded. God, you have been Jehovah Jireh, my Provider, for as long as I've known you. I trust you now in this crisis that I am currently experiencing. I will not waiver in my faith because your word says in Hebrews 11:6, *But without faith, it is impossible to please Him, for He who comes to God must believe that He is and that He is a rewarder of those who diligently seek Him.* God, I thank you in advance for healing my mom and supplying all of my needs according to your riches in glory in Christ Jesus (Philippians 4:19); Thank you, Father, for providing for my family in Jesus' Name, Amen."

After Karen finished praying, she fed her children and told them there's no school for a while, explaining why. Her eight-year-old daughter got up from the table, proceeded to her room, and started crying. After consoling her, Karen was exhausted. When the night quieted down, she received a phone call from her sister, sobbing, as she had just received the disturbing news about their mother. Her sister then began to blame Karen for not telling her immediately about her mom. As Karen started explaining to her sister that she had just found out, she felt the peace of God come upon her and soon ended the conversation.

Karen woke up praying to God each morning, similarly to the prayer she had said the previous day. Then she would work on her job applications. After several days, Karen received a call from her aunt telling her that her mother passed away from pneumonia. Upon hearing this terrible news, Karen dropped the phone and was speechless! She went numb! Karen's sisters tried to call her repeatedly, but was unable to reach her. When she'd finally gathered her bearings, the phone rang again, and it was her sisters on the phone; they all began to weep. One of her sisters commented that God is not fair and said that she had lost trust in Him a long time ago. "How could He let this happen to Momma?" she asked, her voice breaking.

Karen reminded her sister that God allows things but assured her that He did not cause their mother to die. Karen, knowing that her sister battled with alcoholism, reminded her how God kept her alive when she crashed into a tree after driving drunk. She began to think about the teachings of her mom and shared them with her sisters. Karen reminded them both that mom lived a wonderful life and was now 80 years old. She began to quote the scriptures found in Ecclesiastes 3:1-4: *For everything, there is a season, and a time for every purpose under heaven: a time to be born, and a time to die; a time to plant, and a time to pluck up that which is planted; a time to kill, and a time to heal; a time to break down, and a time to build up; a time to weep, and a time to laugh; a time to mourn, and a time to dance.*

They all spoke the next day, along with their aunt and the funeral directors, to plan a Livestream Memorial for their mom, which was also very difficult for them. Karen said words of honor and encouragement for the Memorial Service. Her mom had confounded the doctors due to her sharing her faith with them during her mother's illness. Being very intrigued, her sisters attended the service as well. At the end of the service, one of Karen's sisters vowed her life to Christ, as did one of the doctors. All three siblings promised to talk more, and visit more, once the pandemic is over.

You see, at some point in many of our lives, we are confronted with obstacles and even devastating news when we are most vulnerable. However, we have the choice to either blame God or trust Him in everything. We must realize that just like God brought Karen and her siblings back together, saved her sister's soul, blessed Karen with another job a week later, He is always working behind the scenes. Although it was not the answer Karen wanted, God had even answered her prayer about confounding the doctors. Romans 8:28 states, *And we know that all things work together for the good of them who love the Lord, who are the called according to His purpose.* We must remember our ways are not His ways and our thoughts are not His thoughts.

I know it's tough to see the good in dark times or seasons in your life, but trusting God, pleases Him. Remember Karen's prayer? She thanked God during her storm, and she trusted Him. Just like our natural parents, when we please them, we are rewarded. It may not seem like a reward to have a loved-one taken, but to be absent in the body is to be present with the Lord; the ultimate prize! What are you asking from God? Know that He is attentive to your cry. I encourage you to keep the faith.

Day 1: A Time of Reflection and Renewal

What is one takeaway that I have from today's reading?

_____

_____

_____

How does this impact me spiritually and emotionally?

_____

_____

_____

After my reading of Day 1, what practical steps can I take for a more positive outcome? _____

_____

_____

_____

What impact will this have on me, my family and others?

_____

_____

_____

DAY 2

Jesus Saves

Amy made her way to the altar after hearing a sermon preached, *Jesus Loves Me This I Know*. She recalled when she was a little girl, and her mother taught her that song and how it came to be her favorite song. However, Amy grew up in a volatile home with constant bickering and fighting between her mother and father. One day, when she was six years old, her father left home and never turned back.

Amy's mother did not show her love, affection, and attention as she showed her two younger siblings. As a result, Amy grew up with episodes of anger and depression. She felt like the family's black sheep and ran away from home at the age of thirteen. A week later, she was raped and left for dead. A Good Samaritan saw Amy lying unconscious on a dark road and took her to a nearby hospital where they contacted Amy's mother. She moved back home with her mother and a new stepfather. Amy began to suffer from PTSD (Post Traumatic Stress Disorder) along with depression. However, Amy's parents continued to show more attention to her sister and brother. Although Amy was always an honor roll student, she began failing in school due to her lack of psychological and emotional support and became promiscuous with older boys. She ran away again at the age of fifteen.

Amy became pregnant at sixteen and quit school. She began working and moved in with her boyfriend. In time, Amy gave birth to a beautiful baby girl. She became estranged from her family and continued to live with her boyfriend as they both worked very hard to support their daughter. At the age of eighteen, Amy began battling with anger, depression, and symptoms of PTSD again. Amy never resolved her issues. She felt rejection and abandonment by her father and her mother. Amy did not know how it felt to be loved by her parents. Neither did she know how to communicate her feelings. At this point, her baby's father left her.

It wasn't until Amy was invited to church by a co-worker when she heard the Pastor preaching *Jesus Loves Me This I Know*, she explained to her friend that she had an overwhelming feeling of emotions that came over her. "I felt at that moment that someone more significant than any individual on earth loves me. God loves me." Amy remembered the scripture read by the pastor, John 3:16 - *For God so loved the world that he gave His only begotten son, that whosoever believes in Him shall not perish but have everlasting life.* Amy made her way to the altar as the congregation began to sing, *Jesus loves me this I know, for the Bible tells me so, little ones to Him belong, they are weak, but He is strong. Yes, Jesus Loves Me, yes Jesus loves me. Yes, Jesus loves me, for the Bible tells me so.*

Amy repented, accepted Jesus Christ as her Lord and Savior, and joined the church. Amy was discipled by a small group of ladies in their twenties and thirties, who had a commitment and relationship with God. She was introduced to a counselor and faithfully attended her therapy sessions. Amy forgave her parents, was healed, and became a disciple to others a few years later. After a while, she met a young man at her church, got married, and had another baby girl. Amy earned her high school diploma, enrolled in college, and pursued a bachelor's degree in social work. It wasn't a bed of roses for Amy once she gave her life to Christ, but she was willing and committed. Amy learned the power of prayer and that God will never leave or forsake her. Her faith had increased ten-fold.

You may or may not be able to relate to Amy somehow, but one thing I do know is we all were lost and needed a savior at some point in our lives. You may not have had a horrific childhood, traumatic experiences, rejection, or abandonment, but you still need a Savior. Psalm 51:5 states, *Behold, I was shapen in iniquity; and in sin did my mother conceive me.* Romans 3:23 states, *For all have sinned and fall short of the glory of God.* However, I'm so glad that Jesus Christ found it not robbery to purchase us back by dying on the Cross for our sins. He didn't just die; He was buried and rose again with all power in His hands.

Romans 8:34 states, *It is Christ who died and furthermore is also risen, who is even at the right hand of God, who also makes intercession for us*. As Amy was going through her struggles, Jesus was there the entire time talking to God about Amy, pleading her case to God, asking him not to let her die with her sins unrepentant. Can you believe Jesus does that for us every day? Thank you Jesus!

Amid our sins, God still loves us; we discover He was there all the time. Romans 5:8 tell us, *God demonstrates His own love towards us, in that while we were yet sinners, Christ died for us.* There is absolutely nothing you can do to stop God from loving you. The only thing that separates us from God is sin. But again, that doesn't stop God from loving you. Remember the message Amy heard from John 3:16?

If you have not accepted Jesus as your Lord and Savior, today is your day. Romans 10:9 states, *if you confess with your mouth the Lord Jesus and believe in your heart that God has raised Him from the dead, you will be saved.*

Day 2: A Time of Reflection and Renewal

Is there a time I've had regrets about? Can I repent and let it go? _____

_____

_____

How can releasing my past impact me spiritually and emotionally?_____

_____

_____

Am I ready to commit my life to God? What's holding me back?" _____

_____

_____

What impact will this have on me, my family and others?

_____

_____

_____

DAY 3

That Is Not My Name

Dante, also known as "No Good," chose to erase the stigma and name given to him at a very young age. Dante's single mother raised him and his three siblings. Dante was the second oldest of his mother's children. Dante and his siblings never met their father as he was in and out of jail and is currently serving a life sentence in prison. Dante struggled academically in school but was very talented in sports, such as football, basketball, baseball, and running track. Also, Dante possessed a gift of poetry, which he kept to himself. Many did not know, including his family.

Growing up in an urban neighborhood, everyone knew each other. Dante's father was the "All-Star" champion of sports at the local middle and high school but always had behavioral issues. When Dante entered third grade, he struggled academically, and negative behaviors manifested similar to his father's. Dante was involved in many fights. One particular day, his math teacher said to him, "You are 'No Good's' son; you are going to be no good just like your father." Dante looked the teacher in the eyes and said, "No, I will not," in a very stern tone. Dante never told his mother about this incident because he didn't want to upset her, but he was determined to be better than his father.

Throughout his school-aged years, Dante continued to fight, but only if he had to defend himself. Dante's mother was very frustrated since the school called her numerous times to pick up Dante after being suspended. When Dante was fourteen years old, he got into a fight and broke the other boy's nose. Dante faced expulsion from school and spent a month in the juvenile detention center. When his mother came to pick him up, she yelled at him and said, "you are no good just like your no-good daddy . . . that was his nickname, and from now on, that is your name, No Good!" Dante immediately had a flashback from the third grade, when his math teacher had thrown the same name at him. He looked his mother in her eyes as they filled with anger, disappointment, and tears, and yelled back at her, "That is Not My Name!"

When Dante left the detention center, he was determined not to live up to the name "No Good." But when he went back to school, the teachers and students referred to him as "No Good," as if that was an acceptable name for him. Dante went to the principal to complain, only to hear, "prove that is not your name." Dante was upset that the principal did not stop the teachers from calling him that name. However, from that day forward, Dante's life changed.

Dante did not play sports for the rest of his freshman nor sophomore year. Instead, he stayed after school for tutoring, improved his grades, and changed his behavior. Dante was still being called "No Good" at school and occasionally at home, whenever his mom was upset with him. When Dante entered the eleventh grade, he began playing sports again and continued to make average grades. Dante began to write more and more poetry, which allowed him to express his powerful emotions. He began reciting his poetry at the school's talent shows, which soon became known as "Open Mic" for the inner-city youth. Open Mic became a place where children could go to have fun and be safe on Friday nights at the school.

One night Dante was taking friends home from Open Mic and was stopped by a police officer. Dante asked the officer why he pulled him over, and the officer proceeded to ask for his driver's license and proof of insurance. Immediately after looking at his name, the officer began to say, "you are . . . " and Dante said, "That is Not My Name." The officer walked away to check Dante's license. When he returned to the car asking all of the boys to step out, all four boys politely stepped out of the car with their hands raised in the air. The officer patted them down and searched the vehicle. When the officer saw that the boys were clean, he said to Dante, "You're right, that's not your name and don't ever let that be your name; young men, you are free to go . . . and by the way, Dante, get your tail light fixed."

Dante graduated from high school and received a scholarship to attend college. Dante was the first in his family to attend college. He graduated with a Bachelor's Degree in Psychology and returned to his home town to be a Counselor. Dante also started an Inner-City Youth Program, including tutoring, counseling, sports, mentoring, and his famous "Open Mic." Dante continues to mentor at-risk youth and has turned around over two-hundred lives. The high school graduation rate in his town went from 65% to 90%. Many of the youth went to college, started their businesses, or enlisted in the military. Many of our children and us have and continue to be labeled by our parents and family members. The negative name was a physical seed planted genetically by Dante's father and his teacher at a tender age, and of course, his mother. Not every child can fight the temptations, the physical and mental torture of behaving in a way that seems to be part of their genetic make-up. It is also difficult for anyone, especially a child, to be continuously reminded of this fact and made to feel like they have no other choice but to be this way, despite standing up and saying "No."

No matter where you come from, what your parents, grandparents, or other family members have done, it does not have to define who you are. Jeremiah 1:5 states, *Before I formed you in the womb, I knew you; before you were born I sanctified you; I ordained you a prophet to the nations.*

Just like God ordained Jeremiah as a Prophet, God has ordained each of His children to be something great. It may be a part of the Five-Fold Ministry (Apostle, Prophet, Evangelist, Pastor or Teacher), or a counselor, mentor, psychologist, psychiatrist, doctor, lawyer, engineer, nurse, human resources professional, star athlete, poet, author, entrepreneur, or a political figure and any other designation. Whatever it may be, God ordained it. When you walk in your God-given purpose, your "name," which He has given you, will be blessed, and you will be a blessing to others. Jeremiah 29:11 states, *For I know the thoughts that I think toward you says the LORD, thoughts of peace and not of evil, to give you a future and a hope.* This scripture alone should give you a sense of purpose.

If you are living a life from any of these circumstances: generational cycles, mother and father wounds, brought up with lies whispered in your ears from the devil (who is your enemy), always hearing labels about who you are and what others say you would be, know that Satan gave you a name that is NOT the name God has given you. It is time to tell the devil and anyone who has called you a name other than what God has given you, "That is Not My Name!" Proverbs 18:21 states, *Death and Life is in the power of the tongue, and those who love it will eat of it's fruit.* The fruit is the manifestation of what and who you think you are.

Day 3: A Time of Reflection and Renewal

What is one takeaway that I have from today's reading?
_____

_____

_____

Has anyone labeled me, such as my family, a teacher, or a friend? Have I labeled myself? _____

_____

_____

If I ignore what criticisms people have of me, how would that impact my self-esteem?_____

_____

_____

Are there other people I know that I can help after restoring the sense of myself as loved by God? _____

_____

_____

DAY 4

Take Control Of Your Mental Health

Grace is a wife and mother of three. She is a full-time Accountant at a CPA firm and a small business owner performing taxes and other accounting services. Grace is very involved in her church, where she volunteers with community outreach on several levels. She was also the team mom captain for her daughter's girls' softball team.

After twenty years of wearing many hats, Grace began experiencing a burn-out. Also, Grace started having anxiety, insomnia, and became short-tempered. She explained to her husband, who works in Public Health, how she was feeling. Her husband advised her to give up some of her responsibilities. Grace did not want to take her husband's advice because she honored her commitments. Therefore, she continued to live her life according to her current norms until one day she felt sharp pains in her chest and down her left arm and numbness and tingling in her hands. Grace rushed to the hospital, where doctors ran tests and concluded that Grace had a mild stroke and had developed high blood pressure.

Grace realized that she should have taken her husband's advice but did not know how to balance her life. But while she was in the hospital, Grace met a nurse who told her about a therapist who could help her with family/work/life balance.

Grace started attending therapy sessions and realized her life became imbalanced. She was a "busy" woman and had a problem with saying no to others' demands. Not only was her physical health suffering, but her mental health was suffering as well, which was a direct correlation with her insomnia, anxiety, and the other issues listed above.

Knowing that she had to change if she wanted to survive, live a healthy life and continue to be successful, she started walking every morning, which helped her clear her head. Grace began praying more, reading and meditating on the Word of God. She also took a much-needed summer vacation from her business, and her husband took her to Hawaii for a week's vacation. She also took another week off to have a vacation from the vacation. Grace sat out from her girls' softball team for the next season and obtained more assistance in her responsibilities in the outreach program at church. Grace was a new woman. She was more productive at work, church, and even at home. She learned that she couldn't be everything to everybody and maintain her sanity and optimal health. Grace even reserved "Me" time every Saturday afternoon.

Isn't it ironic that Grace did not stop and take a break until her physical body experienced symptoms of a breakdown? She started experiencing a mental health break first but ignored it. Often we neglect our mental health due to a lack of education about the importance of recognizing symptoms and caring for our mental health. It is easy to overextend ourselves. However, it is vital to learn balance to maintain optimum physical and psychological health. Mental health has such a stigma that people suffer and fail to get the help they need. Even if you suspect you are mentally or emotionally compromised, don't ignore it. Get the help you need before it spirals out of control.

Sometimes God will allow us to experience a melt-down for us to realize that we need help. 3 John 1:2 states, *Beloved, I wish above all things that you will prosper and be in health even as your soul prospers.* It is not a sin to take a mental health break. God designed our bodies and brains to rest. After God finished with creation, He rested (Genesis 2:2). Our mental health also affects our physical health. When we are healthy mentally, we have more energy to be more physically active. We can think clearly and be alert. 1 Peter 5:8 tells us to *be sober, be vigilant; because your adversary, the devil, walks about like a roaring lion, seeking whom he may devour.* We must be alert to see the enemy and be in an excellent posture to fight against his attacks. When our minds are healthy, we develop and maintain healthy relationships; we can give back to our communities, be useful to God, and successfully pursue our destiny. Choose today to take control of your mental health. Reach out to a therapist or counselor. Don't suppress your emotions, from whatever source they come. Conquer your fears. Let go of anxiety, the pressures of life, your past, or anything that keeps you up at night or makes you restless and anxious. Become a healthier you!

Day 4: A Time of Reflection and Renewal

Is there an area in my life right now where I am overwhelmed?
_____
_____
_____

What would be the result of me saying No when I need physical and mental rest? _____
_____
_____

When was the time in my past when I pushed myself so hard I became ill? _____
_____
_____

How would my life improve if I share or delegate some of my responsibilities?_____
_____
_____
_____

DAY 5

The Power To Succeed

Gia struggled to complete her education. She graduated from high school and got pregnant with her oldest daughter, who was stillborn. She was utterly devastated. She moved with her mentor, who encouraged Gia to pursue her college degree and walked her through many failures and challenges in her life. Gia was side-tracked by her first husband's lifestyle that was different from hers. Gia and her husband finally divorced after having a very financially and emotionally challenging marriage for Gia.

Gia had her oldest son and daughter by the age of twenty-two and decided to pursue her education. Gia finished all of her general education courses but struggled to do so. She had to take her children (ages two and five) to class with her at night, as they sat quietly at a desk in the back of the classroom, sometimes drawing on paper and other times falling asleep. She would also drive over 350 miles in one day to attend college on Saturdays for a semester. With all of the challenges, Gia maintained a 3.6. GPA and was inducted into the Alpha Sigma Lambda National Honor Society. Did I say it was easy for Gia? It was not! However, she took courage in knowing that the struggle was worth it for her and her children. Not only did she want her education for a better job, but she also wanted to set a standard and bar for her children to one day exceed. Between being a mom, juggling relationship challenges, marriage, divorce, working full-time—and at times, part-time—she took a break from school. She had another child and wondered: what am I going to do now? After she had her baby boy, she began taking online classes to continue her education. In less than a year, she finished and obtained her AA degree. She started a side business doing secretarial work, so she no longer had to work two jobs away from home. Eventually, Gia became very successful in finding employment and continued to work her business. Should I say Gia was a bonafide legal hustler who had the drive to succeed? Later, Gia obtained her bachelor's and master's degrees and received promotions to leadership positions in her secular roles. It was a twenty-year journey from graduating from high school to earning her master's degree, but she did it! She never fell below a 3.5 GPA as she pursued her education, but it did take sacrifice, hard work, and dedication.

Gia is a product of a single-family home with an absent father. She had a rocky ride as a child and even as an adult. Gia faced homelessness numerous times, went without lights and water, and even got down to only beanies and weenies with her little ones. However, she possessed the power to succeed. She knew that life was not a fairy tale; it was real. Gia tells many that it was God who carried her through the darkest times. She says, "He knew my struggle, but He also knows my faith and determination." She is very successful today, and her children are employed and have plans to pursue their education, entrepreneurship, and the military. Gia has and continues to encourage as many people to pursue their education and careers.

As with Gia, no matter what obstacle you may face, you possess the power on the inside for you to succeed. Philippians 4:13 states, I can do all things through Christ who strengthens me. You see, God gives us power through Holy Spirit to chase our dreams, overcome our fears, beat our obstacles and conquer what often appears to be impossible. Whatever you may have put on the back burner or feel that you can't do because you're too old, you're too tired, it's too late, you're not just the right one for this, but you can be ripe for this! I encourage you to put a stake in the ground and tell the enemy: *With God, all things are possible* (Matthew 19:26). You may have to declare those very words to yourself. Many times we are our worst enemies. However, it's not over until God says it's over or when you stop trying!

Go back to school, start that business, create that new invention, write your book, repair your credit, buy that home, take the promotion, chase your dreams. You have the Power to Succeed!

Day 5: A Time of Reflection and Renewal

Is there somewhere in my life where I feel I have failed?
_____
_____
_____

Can I forgive myself? Do I have the courage to make changes?
_____
_____
_____

What would be my first step in accomplishing my dream?
_____
_____
_____

Can I trust that the Lord will help me move toward my goals?
_____
_____
_____

DAY 6

Am I Living Or Existing?

Have you ever walked through life wondering, Where am I? What am I doing? Well, that was Cashmere aka "Cash." Cash, now forty years old, was "living it up," as some would say. Growing up, she was a beautiful young lady with a nice figure whom all the boys loved. She had it going on, and she knew it. However, she didn't know that she lived life as if she didn't have a life. Her grandmother raised her since her mother died in a tragic car accident when she was nine years old. She was an only child and given everything she wanted from her grandmother. Cash participated in beauty pageants, in dancing competitions, in the church choir, Girl Scouts, and made excellent school grades.

However, at age sixteen, Cash started smoking marijuana, drinking alcohol and became promiscuous with boys and girls. Cash became very disrespectful to her grandmother, who tried to guide her in the direction that would lead her to her ultimate success. Her grandmother knew about banking and investing. Cash even learned a little about real estate from her grandmother, a realtor, and knew about God. Eventually, Cash had a free ride to college on an academic scholarship. But she dropped out of college her sophomore year. Cash became addicted to prescription drugs. She was found unconscious by a friend in her apartment but made it through this crisis alive. I mean, she was breathing again!

In time, Cash got a job at the County Library in her hometown, where she had enough income to keep up her apartment, vehicle, and other expenses. Cash's grandmother passed away when Cash was twenty-five years old, yet she didn't know how to grieve her grandmother's death. She continued in her promiscuous lifestyle, smoking marijuana and hanging out at bars. By the time Cash turned thirty, she was abusing prescription drugs again and arrested for narcotics possession. She spent six months in jail and attended a diversion program. The judge withheld adjudication and gave her one year of probation.

While Cash was in jail, she woke up one day out of living a life that had spiraled out of control and asked herself, what am I doing with my life? She finally realized the person who was so dear to her had lived a great life and had raised her to do the same. She woke up to the fact that this person was now gone. She realized that the decision to change the trajectory of her path was only up to her. Without her grandmother's encouragement, she would have to save herself.

Cash committed herself to a treatment center and stayed there for six months. While she was there, she attended therapy and revealed that she didn't know what life was all about. She felt as if she was just "having fun and living it up." Her mom died, and her grandmother kept her very busy to keep her mind off of her mother's death. Cash expressed that she was going through an identity crisis because she didn't have a mother or father in her life, neither did she see or hear about relationships at home. She never knew her grandfather, and her grandmother never talked about him.

Cash was able to grab hold of her life. She started to attend church again, rededicated her life to God, and is now married. She had her 1st child at age thirty-seven. Sadly, Cash found out that she was HIV positive during her pregnancy with her daughter. She and her husband separated, but they are now back together. Cash became a licensed realtor and is pursuing her degree in business management.

Many times we are handed the short end of the stick, dealt a bad hand, and subsequently made unhealthy decisions in our lives, and we may even feel like Cash: we're "living it up." Cash was living but was lifeless. She was a beautiful little girl who became lost in the shadow of a storm that swept her into a place she never dreamed she would be. Cash's life was on fast-forward and without genuine emotions; living without a pulse. Was she really living? Besides giving Cash pretty much everything she wanted, the biggest mistake her grandmother made was not allowing her to grieve her mother's death. It could be that she had unanswered questions.

Where are you today? Are you in touch with yourself? Have you adequately grieved the loss of a love-one? Have you suffered the loss of a relationship? Have you come to terms with the poor decisions you've made in order to move forward? Are you stuck in a place where you last knew yourself? Are you living, or are you just existing? If you live your life without adequately dealing with your past or current issues, and you've opted to numb the pain by using or abusing any form of drugs, alcohol, sex, or by self-sabotaging, know that you still have a life that is worth living. Now is the time to wake up out of your slumber and find the help you need!

I know sin feels good! I thought I was "living life" when I was searching for love in all the wrong places... medicating my hurt and emotions with sex. I thought a man was the best thing for me; I felt I was living, but I was merely existing. Cash was merely existing as well. Some of you who are currently reading this are only existing. The enemy wants your life, your health, your strength, your destiny! He wants you dead! John 10:10 states, the thief comes to steal, kill and destroy, but Jesus tells us in John 10:11, *I come that they may have life and they may have it more abundantly.* Would you believe me when I tell you that God has greatness for you? Yes, He does! *God knows the thoughts He thinks towards us, and it's not of evil or to harm us but to give us hope and a future* (Jeremiah 29:11).

My friend, you can't live this life without Jesus. Jesus said *I am the way, the truth, and the life* (John 14:6). God will deliver you from your struggles and addictions, no matter how hard they may seem to be. There was a woman in the Bible with an issue of blood for twelve long years, who spent everything she had on doctors who could not help her. But while Jesus was passing by getting ready to perform a miracle, she knew that if she could just make her way in the crowd and touch the hem of his garment, she would be made whole. Guess what? She touched him, and immediately Jesus felt the virtue leave His body as He made her whole. She would not have received healing and wholeness if she didn't have faith!

1 John 1:9 states *If we confess our sins, God is faithful and just to forgive and cleanse us from all unrighteousness.* Confess your sins to God today. He wants to make you whole. God also gives us doctors and therapists. If you need to go to a treatment center, Go. If you need to see a doctor or a psychiatrist, Go. If you need counseling, see a therapist. If you need to see a spiritual leader, talk to your Pastor or Minister. It is best to go to someone confidential and trustworthy.

Day 6: A Time of Reflection and Renewal

Have I had any losses in my life that I have not worked through and sufficiently grieved? _____

_____

_____

How can I ask for help from God to carry me through my grief?

_____

_____

_____

Are there ways that I avoided my grief that resulted in abuse or addiction?_____

_____

_____

Can I give up what is bad for me and substitute an addiction for prayer and God? _____

_____

_____

DAY 7

Get Off The Merry-Go-Round

Sometimes life can resemble kids playing on a merry-go-round. Alice took a seat at the park with her two grandchildren, and they immediately raced to get on the swings. They appeared to be enjoying themselves but just on the other side of the swings was a merry-go-round. Suddenly about four other little ones ran and jumped onto it with excitement, and a teenager ran it for them. Alice's grandchildren went over to join the group of children on the merry-go-round because it appeared to be more exciting than the swings. It was fast, fun, it made the children laugh, and they didn't want to stop. They yelled one after another, "do it again" . . . and again . . . and again, until the teen became tired. He took a break and told the children to take a break as well.

Alice called her grandchildren over and gave them something to drink. They returned to the other children, and the six little ones began to chase each other running in circles until the teen returned. They quickly jumped into that cycle of moving in circles. They were supercharged and ready to go on the merry-go-round again. And again and again, they went, yelling "faster . . . faster." They were wearing the young man out as he ran around in circles pulling the merry-go-round with his every move. As she watched the children closely, Alice noticed that her six-year-old granddaughter was holding on very quietly and didn't appear to be doing well. Alice rushed over and asked the teenager to stop the merry-go-round. As she reached for her granddaughter, the little girl immediately began to vomit and then appeared lethargic. Alice laid her on the ground and the teen brought over a cool paper towel to put on her forehead.

Her granddaughter shortly started to feel better but complained that she had a headache as they left the park. Alice explained to her two grandchildren that the merry-go-round might be a fun piece of equipment for children, but it is not good to continue going around in circles at a fast pace for an extended period of time. Alice's grandson asked her, "if it's not good for children, why is it at the park?" She explained that it is there because it's fun for the children, but it is to be used with caution, as it can also cause harm.

She told them that sometimes you have to get off the merry-go-round because it can cause you to become dizzy, lightheaded, nauseous, and even pass out. Alice said, you're moving, but you're not going anywhere. Alice's granddaughter said she doesn't want to get on a merry-go-round ever again, while her brother said, "I do . . . I had so much fun moving and not going anywhere." Alice chuckled and said, "you just said a mouthful, little boy." Just in that quick moment, she remembered living her life at some point as if she was on a merry-go-round.

Many of us have lived our lives on a merry-go-round. In the beginning, we're having fun and find it exciting. We get the rush of jumping off and on, repeatedly, faster and faster. Finally, we realize that time continues to move with or without us.

Like Alice's grandson, we don't want to stop because we become accustomed to that lifestyle and become almost like the energizer bunny, circling around and around, until we begin to experience motion sickness. How does that look? Just like Alice's granddaughter. However, when we experience spiritual motion sickness, we don't have time to hear from God or anyone else. Our heads are spinning, and we can't see; we can barely talk. Sometimes it takes our breath away, and we continue to do the same thing repeatedly, which is insane, but our immunity to the motion blinds us. As they say, insanity is doing the same thing over and over again but expecting a different result each time. When does it stop?

Alice had her share of merry-go-rounds, but she finally realized that while life may have appeared to be different as if changes were occurring, it was the same thing but just a new day. That's what happens when you're on a merry-go-round. She was not moving or progressing on a divine path, but just going through the motions, as she had been accustomed to living her life in cycles, defeated, as a victim, a worrier, a pretender, and the list goes on. This syndrome of experience is called the "merry-go-round."

If you find yourself on a merry-go-round, I implore you today to stop it and get off. God is a God of progression, not a God who circles in place. Psalm 23:2 states, He leads me beside the still waters. There was forward movement. As King David allowed God to guide him, God was able to still the waters, which gave King David peace, and God was able to restore his soul (Psalm 23:3). Though I walk through the valley of the shadow of death, King David said, I will fear no evil (Psalm 23:4) because God's rod and staff comforted him. Again, King David was on the move, even though he was in a dark time in his life. He kept it moving as he said *Surely goodness and mercy shall follow me all the days of my life.* King David didn't cycle. King David would not have become King, which was God's purpose and plan for His life—if he was on a merry-go-round. King David had every right to get on one and take his enemies on a ride with him when Saul and his other enemies pursued him. Instead, King David allowed God to order His steps, which resulted in him becoming a great King and a mighty warrior, although he was not a perfect man.

Day 7: A Time of Reflection and Renewal

What is one takeaway that I have from today's reading?
_____
_____
_____

Is there a place in my life where I am running in circles?
_____
_____
_____

Can I stand still long enough to see where I intend to go?
_____
_____
_____

What steps can I take to begin my divine path?_____
_____
_____
_____

DAY 8

God Is Still In Control

It is nice to sit down and conveniently flip from channel to channel to pick whatever you want to watch on television. There is practically a remote control for most electronic devices now. You can turn on, turn off, change channels, change stations, increase and decrease volumes, go to a menu to select various settings and options, and the list goes on. We love the convenience, and we love the control. What happens when we lose the remote? I already know; I can hear the sigh, the thump in your heart! We flip madly over pillows, chairs, sofas, get on our hands and knees, and then the blame game begins! It is always someone else who lost the remote, never you. I am chuckling right now because I can relate. How far is the television? I would guess probably just a few feet away. How far is the radio, the computer, the other devices? Why do we flip out or get upset when we or someone else has misplaced, not lost, the remote? It's all because we lose our control.

Many times, on our journey in life, our homes, children, marriages, schools, government, jobs, the economy, law enforcement, deadlines, and much more lose control! What happened? Did someone lose the remote? Who lost control? That very thing that seems to keep our lives on track is gone. Is it our minds? Is it our faith? Is it our integrity? Is it our love? Is it our compassion? Is it our respect? Whatever it may be, the problem and its consequences revolve around some type of control and the loss thereof. I can assure you that God is still in control, even in the midst of a national pandemic, the novel Coronavirus (COVID-19), which has killed over two-hundred thousand Americans and over one million individuals nationwide. He is still in control even amidst the current breaking news that has reached worldwide regarding the senseless, heinous murder of a black man committed by a white cop in Minneapolis, who knelt on his neck for almost 10 minutes after he was already detained (handcuffed).

When "We" lose control, God never loses control. Psalm 138:6 states, *Yet the Lord is on high, He regards the lowly, but the proud he knows afar.* This is the scripture that we commonly quote as God sits high and looks low, meaning nothing catches him by surprise—He sees all. Psalm 37:1 states, *Fret not yourselves because of evildoers, nor be envious of the workers of iniquity. For they soon shall be cut down like the grass and wither as the green herb.* Deuteronomy 32:35 states, *Vengeance is mine, and I will repay. Their foot shall slip in due time. For the day of calamity is at hand. And the things to come hasten upon them.*

I encourage you to trust God (who is Supreme over everyone and everything), to control what we absolutely cannot control. He doesn't cause evil, but He certainly will take the evil and turn it around for our good! Romans 8:28 states, *And we know that all things work together for the good of them who love the Lord and who are the called according to His purpose.* God delivered the children of Israel out of the hands of Pharaoh and the Egyptian Army, who drowned in the Red Sea. God will also deliver His people from racism and racial division, injustice, deadly viruses, economic crisis, loss of jobs, and whatever you've lost control over today and every day. God is the same today, yesterday, and forever! Know that when we cannot conveniently cause things to happen with the click of a button, God can! He is Still in Control!

Day 8: A Time of Reflection and Renewal

Can I relate to today's reading on losing the remote? _____

_____

_____

_____

Is there a place in my life that feels out of control?_____

_____

_____

_____

How do I feel about the current state of the world?

_____

_____

_____

Are there areas in my life where I could create more control by uniting with others? _____

_____

_____

_____

DAY 9

I Need Help

Rosa's husband John, recently hurt his back from a severe fall at work, which required surgery. Both Rosa and John are in their mid-sixties. They have two married daughters who have their own families, but they consistently call and check on their parents. Since John's injury, Rosa continues to take care of the domestic chores and musters up enough strength to move heavy items, mow the lawn, and take care of other tasks that her husband would typically handle. Each time their daughters and sons-in-law reached out to them and asked how they could help, they both said they did not need help.

While re-organizing the garage one day, Rosa attempted to move a large gas can full of gas. She felt a rip in her shoulder, after which she immediately felt excruciating pain in her shoulder, which radiated down her arms. Rosa called her daughters, and one of them took her to the emergency room, while the other met them at the hospital. Both daughters were upset with their mom for not asking for help. Rosa tore her rotator cuff, which resulted in surgery, and was also undergoing a slow and painful recovery. Now, both parents were down and needed assistance. John waited on Rosa to recover from her surgery before having his. John suffered from back pain for an additional eight weeks. John and Rosa's daughters and their husbands took turns assisting them daily. John and Rosa realized that they were very prideful and could have avoided the unnecessary injuries, expenses, and logistical changes to their lifestyle if they only would have agreed to receive help when asked.

Similarly, we try to live our lives without God. We allow pride to get in the way. We indulge our selfish will instead of submitting to the will of God for our benefit. Sometimes accidents happen to make us slow down and pay attention to what our bodies need. It is impossible to live successful lives without God! It often appears that we are successful. However, if we were completely honest, we can admit that there are so many broken areas in our lives. Instead of surrendering to God, who will forgive, heal, deliver and set free, provide, protect, rule, mend, restore, and anything else we could ever imagine, we would try to do everything on our own and fail hopelessly. We often live our lives without having God's best plan He has for us. Finally, we decide to come to God when we are broke down, busted, and disgusted. Yes, He will always be there, but why not consult him first? Why not obey him first? Why not save ourselves from so much unnecessary pain and drama? It is high time to say out loud, "I Need Help!" Husbands, wives, children, extended family, our cities, counties, government, and the world need God's help.

King David said it best in Psalm 121, *I will lift up mine eyes unto the hills, from whence cometh my help, my help cometh from the Lord, which made heaven and earth. He will not suffer thy foot to be moved: he that keepeth thee will not slumber. Behold, he that keepeth Israel shall neither slumber nor sleep. The Lord is thy keeper: the Lord is thy shade upon thy right hand. The sun shall not smite thee by day, nor the moon by night. The Lord shall preserve thee from all evil: he shall preserve thy soul. The Lord shall preserve thy going out and thy coming in from this time forth, and even forevermore.*

I encourage you today to ask God to take you to a new level, make you complete in Him, order your steps, make a change in your life, and show you how to be a change agent. Say it with me: "I Need Help!"

Day 9: A Time of Reflection and Renewal

What is one takeaway that I have from today's reading about Rosa and John?_____

_____

_____

Do I know of anyone who should have asked for help but didn't? _____

_____

_____

How do situations spiral out of control because of having too much pride? _____

_____

_____

_____

Is there somewhere in my life I could and should reach out for help? _____

_____

_____

_____

DAY 10

The Joy Of The Lord

Have you ever met someone who is always joyful when you see them, and you wonder why they keep a smile on their face? Well, this is true for Gabby. Gabby has always been a joyful person, even as a child. Gabby is a breath of fresh air to all who meet her and come to know her. Unfortunately, Gabby's life subjected her to become Satan's target as he tried early in her life to destroy the core of who she was by using other children, who didn't understand this bubbly and joyful little girl. As she and her sister walked home from elementary school, she often was chased by a crowd of children bullying and wanting to fight her. During middle school, Gabby was followed home for one and a half miles by a classmate throwing rocks at her, hitting her in the back of her head, her back, arms, and legs, but she refused to turn around and made it home safely. Gabby had done nothing to this girl. It was her joyful state alone which this girl seemed to despise.

Gabby suffered rejection, abandonment, verbal, physical, and emotional abuse. Worst of all, she was violated sexually as a child. However, Gabby never lost her joy. Years later, as a young lady in the workforce, Gabby was ridiculed by a coworker who stated that she did not like her because she was always smiling. Others often misunderstood her as being phony, but many more people admired her joyful personality so much that they named her "Sunshine." In the workplace, even to this day, she is light that others notice and follow. It was not until Gabby had gone through many hurts and disappointments in her life that she realized that despite all the abuse, she still had her natural joy. Gabby doesn't mind sharing that the Joy she has comes from God alone. She is happy to tell anyone, "the world didn't give it to me, and the world can't take it away." Gabby never lost her joy during the most challenging seasons of her life. She had joy even in her tears and sorrows. Sounds crazy, huh?

1 Peter 1:8 talks about "rejoicing with unspeakable joy." Joy is indescribable. It is not happiness, as being happy is conditional; Happiness varies and depends on a given thing, circumstance or situation. But Joy is unshakable. It doesn't matter what you may experience, good or bad. The joy that God gives us is a part of who He is; it's a fruit of the Spirit (Galatians 5:22-23), which is why it is beyond explanation. Joy belongs to all Believers! Psalm 30:5 states, *Weeping may endure for a night, but joy cometh in the morning.* The word "cometh" means it will continue to come, which means that joy is continuous. Hallelujah, this is good news!

Just like with Gabby, to keep your sanity, you need Joy. Joy keeps you alive. It keeps you healthy. Joy will change your perspective. I encourage you not to allow the cares of this world and the tricks of Satan to rob you of your Joy. Satan knows if he can take your joy, you will become weak and hopeless.

Nehemiah 8:10 states *For the joy of the Lord is your strength.* It is your birthright. Take your joy back if you feel you've lost it. It belongs to you.

Day 10: A Time of Reflection and Renewal

What have I learned from Gabby's story? _____

_____

_____

_____

Can I feel joy everyday just for being one of God's children?

_____

_____

_____

Is there a sorrow I've experienced that I can overcome by finding something joyful that came from that sorrowful event?

_____

_____

_____

Can I write down three things to be joyful about every day?

_____

_____

_____

DAY 11

Broken

During my oldest son's childhood, I found it merely impossible to keep anything around without him breaking it. He broke his toys, my appliances, and nearly everything he put his hands on. It wouldn't matter if it were a gift for Christmas, birthday, or "just because," he would break it. I never believed it was intentional. If there was such a thing back then as non-shatter-able drinking glasses, I needed them. I could never find a glass when wanting a drink because they were all broken.

I would get upset throughout the years when my son broke things because, for one thing, replacing the broken items were getting expensive. I would assure him that he would not get another toy, another game, or he could not touch my iron again—or whatever it was—that he had broken. I felt like he was young and unappreciative, like most children. However, during my childhood, I had better take care of every gift and definitely, items in the home. After preaching this repeatedly while raising my children, I figured they would get it once they start spending their money on things. One surprising thing I realized, my son not only broke nearly everything he touched, but he had a knack for fixing things. As he grew older, most of the time, he was able to repair the broken items. Who knew? Sometimes I wondered if he breaks them, just to have an opportunity to try to fix them.

However, some things were just irreparable. I recall thinking if parents were even to attempt to tally up the cost of repayment of items our children have broken or damaged—and the list goes on—the price would be impossible to repay. We just have to chalk it up as part of our parental territory.

When we entered this world, we all were broken. King David said in Psalm 51:5, *Behold I was shapen in iniquity and in sin my mother conceived me.* God gave us the best gift anyone could ever have—His Son, Jesus Christ. John 3:16 states, For God, so loved the world that He gave His only begotten Son, that whosoever believes in Him shall not perish but have everlasting life. I am sure we have broken God's heart countless times. Every time we sin, we break His heart. When we don't trust Him, we break His heart. When we disobey His voice, we break His heart. When we follow the voice of Satan, we break His heart. However, because God loves us unconditionally, He forgives us over and over again. He could easily withdraw His hand from us. Just like parents vow that when their child breaks a toy, they will never buy them that same toy again, God could tell us the same thing. But thank you, God, that He doesn't tell us that we cannot have the gift of salvation.

God is so faithful that He does not leave us in sin, which is why he gave us His only son, Jesus Christ. Romans 6:23 states, *For the wages of sin is death, but the gift of God is eternal life through Jesus Christ our Lord.* God has given us the best Gift. What have we done with His Gift? His Gift is unbreakable! I thank God that He specializes in brokenness. Unlike us, He does not refuse to repair our brokenness. He doesn't throw us away. The Bible tells us that *a broken and contrite heart, He will not despise* (Psalm 51:17).

God wants us to come to Him broken! It is we who feel that we have it all together. God knows that we do not. God is the only one that can put us back together again. God loves us so much that He will allow us to come to a place of brokenness so we can surrender our will to His. God desires to manifest His perfect will in our lives.

The good thing about allowing God to fix our brokenness is that our lives will never be the same. When we buy something from the store and break it, we can't get that same item again. In the same manner, God doesn't want us to be the same. He makes us brand new. King David said in Psalm 51:10, *Create in me a clean heart, Oh God, and renew a right spirit in me.*

If you find yourself lost in sin, hopeless, confused, and feel that you have done all that you possibly can, but nothing has changed for the better, allow God to repair your brokenness today.

Day 11: A Time of Reflection and Renewal

Where can I find the theme of brokenness in my own life?
_____
_____
_____

Is there a place, spiritually and/or emotionally where God has mended a troubled event for me? _____
_____
_____

Is there a time in my life when I relied on myself to mend the broken pieces of my life?_____
_____
_____
_____

Can I ask God to mend my broken pieces? _____
_____
_____
_____

DAY 12

Be Still

Chris and Linda both have hectic lives. Chris is a firefighter, and Linda is a nurse at a local hospital. They both have been working extra shifts due to the current Coronavirus pandemic. When they see each other at home, they are always on the move. However, they both like to communicate with each other regularly about their daily challenges and experiences. Unfortunately, due to the demands of work right now, they have to talk pretty much on the go.

One day, Chris found himself needing attention and affection from his wife. He became very frustrated, as he felt she was not listening to him. As Chris was trying to tell Linda his big challenge of the day, Linda continued to walk around the house, busily tidying up but not hearing what her husband was saying to her. Chris finally said, "Linda, be still," in a stern tone. Linda said to Chris, "Honey, I'm trying to clean up a little, cook, and get myself ready for work." She walked over to him, kissed him, and kept moving. Chris was convinced that his wife was not listening to him and lost the point of the entire conversation. He grabbed her by the hand gently but firmly and said, "Linda, will you just be still for a minute?" She stopped in her tracks and realized that her husband needed her, so she stood still and asked him what was wrong. Chris proceeded to ask her if she heard him say that his close friend didn't survive the terrible fire they fought last weekend and that he witnessed Joe's death; he was unable to save him. Linda knew about the fire, but she didn't ask any questions when he came home unharmed. Now she heard him and was finally listening to him. Chris got choked up, and so did Linda. Chris had her attention.

Often, we get so busy with our daily routines, and God is trying to tell us to be still. We may not be accustomed to communicating with God throughout the hustle and bustle of our days. We may feel like we prayed last night at the usual time or talked to Him this morning, maybe asking for something, but God might just have something to tell you at a different time of the day. He may need to give specific directions or directives about a particular matter, and if we can't be still for just a minute, we may miss it. Often we think we have it all figured out as it relates to prayer and communicating with God. How good is your communication with Him? Do you know when His tone is different? Do you know when He's trying to get your attention? Can you be still for a moment to discern His voice?

Linda thought it was a typical day of conversing with her husband and was comfortable with their communication style, but she missed it this time. Isaiah 55:8 states, *For my thoughts, are not your thoughts, nor are your ways my ways, says the LORD.* We should never get comfortable with the way God communicates with us. God spoke to Moses through a burning bush (Exodus 3:1-4). He spoke to Gideon through a fleece (Judges 6:37-40). God spoke to Saul on the Damascus road through a bright light (Acts 9:1-5). He even spoke to Balaam through a donkey (Numbers 22:1-35). Now, God speaks through a still small voice; He spoke this way to Elijah (1 Kings 19:12). Each of these forms of communication was specifically chosen by God, causing each person to be still. Now God can still you, or you can choose to be still. I don't know about you, but I would instead choose to be still and listen to God. Notice I said *listen*, not just hear God. There is a difference. Listening causes you to be still and be engaged.

I encourage you today always to be open to how God wants to communicate with you. Don't get too busy for God! Don't get complacent with God! We live in a world full of new experiences that we would never have thought of or imagined. God is doing a new thing, and we need to know how He wants us to respond. Isaiah 43:19 states, *Behold, I will do a new thing; now it shall spring forth; shall ye not know it? I will even make a way in the wilderness and rivers in the desert.* God is speaking. Will you "Be Still" just for a moment?

Day 12: A Time of Reflection and Renewal

What is one takeaway that I have from today's reading?
_____

_____

_____

How and when do I listen to God? _____

_____

_____

_____

Do I take time out during the day to be in stillness and allow God to speak to me?_____

_____

_____

Do I pay attention to details as I go about my routine? Is there a time I can remember that God spoke to me in an unusual way?_____

_____

_____

DAY 13

More Than Enough

Roger went to work bright and early on a Friday. His supervisor called him in the office to advise him that the plant he worked at was closing down, as well as ten others nationwide. Subsequently, Roger lost his job immediately after working there for over fifteen years. He dreaded going home to tell his wife. She had been out of work for the past ten months due to a chronic illness. Roger and his wife, Danielle, had four small children. Roger immediately applied for other jobs and applied for unemployment, as he was the sole provider for his home. He had saved more than enough to pay for their next month's expenses with his last check, which included a vacation payout. But the following month, Roger had to use their savings, which covered another month's bills, but Danielle's medical expenses finally depleted it.

Three months went by, and Roger still had not landed employment. He was becoming frustrated because he was no longer able to provide for his family. Then he remembered the scripture: *I have been young, and now am old, yet I have not seen the righteous forsaken, nor his descendants begging bread* (Psalm 37:25). As the oldest child of a single mother, Roger knew the true meaning of this scripture oh too well. He continued to seek employment, pray, take care of his children, and trust God. A few days later, Roger's church family blessed his family financially, and the amount they received was more than enough to pay another month's expenses once again. Roger was very grateful.

The next month, Danielle's health declined even more. She passed away from uterine cancer, leaving Roger grieving and feeling the stress of being responsible for raising his four children alone. Roger did not know what the week would look like for him and his children, but God never skipped a beat of blessings. Roger finally gained employment at a utility plant as the Plant Manager, making more than he was making before losing his other job. What this meant was that Roger would be getting more than enough! Roger knew that because he had Jesus as His Lord and Savior, God would always take care of his family.

I encourage you today to trust God even when it seems like everything has dried up around you. It's important to know that God will always make way for His children. If God caused manna to rain down from heaven for the children of Israel that proved to be more than enough, if Jesus was able to feed five thousand people with two fish and five loaves of bread, which was more than enough, He is more than enough and has more than enough for you.

Roger witnessed God's grace during a time that should've swept him off his feet and what should've caused much lack in his life. I encourage you not to throw in the towel or run to what feels comfortable to feel secure in these times of uncertainty, but put all of your trust in God! 2 Corinthians 12:9 states, *My grace is sufficient for you, for My strength is made perfect in weakness.* God is the most significant and ultimate source. He is indeed more than enough!

Day 13: A Time of Reflection and Renewal

Have I or anyone I know, ever felt I was, or he or she was without enough? _____

_____

_____

Have I ever noticed that God has my back when I have forgotten His presence? _____

_____

_____

Can I make it a part of my routine to pray for God's help?

_____

_____

_____

Can I set up reminders of the Biblical stories where God has intervened for the good? _____

_____

_____

_____

DAY 14

Excluded

Tracy, a beautiful young lady with a winning personality, was raised in New Jersey by her mother and father, without siblings. Tracy often felt excluded from others because her family were Christian. Tracy's classmates would mock her in school, calling her "Glorified Church Girl." Tracy was never welcomed into the "in crowd" of the popular girls.

Tracy went to college and had fallen in love with a young man she met during her sophomore year. She had high hopes to one day marry him and have a family. However, he decided to break off the relationship after six years, as he decided her Christianity and the idea of marriage was no longer for him. Tracy was distraught. Tracy's girlfriends, whom she met in college, were still with their boyfriends. Two of the couples began planning their weddings. They often hung out as couples, but they stopped calling Tracy to hang out with them after her break-up. They didn't want her to feel awkward, so they never talked to her about it. Tracy felt excluded.

After graduate school, Tracy found herself in a place of loneliness. She began to question if Christianity was right for her. Tracy felt different from others and excluded from what appeared to be a "fun life" for others. However, she remained faithful and loyal to her beliefs. She attended church and joined a small group of Christian women in her age group and began to heal.

A few months later, Tracy moved to a new city for a job offer she could not refuse. She had no family there but had friends from college who lived there. They invited her to a gathering at one of their homes. Tracy arrived and greeted everyone, and it appeared to be a fun and friendly atmosphere. They ate, played cards, and conversed. However, some started pulling away into cliques, excluding Tracy. She found herself sitting alone, outside on the patio. Tracy went inside and sat at the bar with the others, and upon her arrival, the conversation stopped. She walked over to another group who had too much to drink and told offensive jokes, so Tracy decided it was time to leave. Tracy went home and felt a little awkward but realized that everyone is different and did not allow it to bother her.

Tracy's friends invited her to go to a local Sports Bar & Grill with some other college friends she had not seen since her undergraduate years in college. They all shared their life's journey since graduation. They were having a lovely time until some gentlemen came up and started talking with them. They laughed and talked for about twenty minutes. Tracy felt a bit uncomfortable. She went to the restroom and came back to find her friends outside smoking marijuana with the same guys. Tracy walked over to say goodbye, and they acted as if it was no big deal. Worse—was the fact that she and her girlfriends had all met up to hang out together, not to hook-up with some random guys. Tracy was upset. While driving home, she began to whisper these words to God: "Thank you, Lord, for saving my soul, and although my friends often exclude me, I realize that you are always with me. I know that I will meet friends here who are just right for me, who share the same beliefs and values. Lord, give me the strength to go through this season of my life where I feel so alone at times. In Jesus Name, Amen." Tracy found out days later that one of her friends from college went in the car with one of the young men who raped her and shoved her to the side of the road.

You may experience moments in your life where you are alone. You may not fit in with the crowd. People may exclude you from parties, events, conversations, and more. John 17:14-16 states, *I have given them Your word; and the world has hated them because they are not of the world, just as I am not of the world. I do not pray that You should take them out of the world, but that You should keep them from the evil one. They are not of the world, just as I am not of the world.* Jesus talks about His disciples being in the world but not *of* the world. They were on assignment, just as we are! However, He prayed that God did not take them out of the world but keep them from Satan. Jesus made it clear that His disciples would be excluded from the evil one. Yes, Satan would try to come up against them, but he could not have them. Tracy could have been with her friend, as a victim of sexual assault as well, and while they intended to exclude her, God was the one who excluded her, on purpose. God is our Protector. He excludes us from danger. He excludes us from people who will not add value to us, but we must obey him.

1 Peter 5:8 states, *Be sober, and be vigilant; because your adversary the devil walks about like a roaring lion, seeking whom he may devour.* It may appear like Satan has access to us, our family, and our personal belongings, but he only has access to what we give him or what God allows. Satan tries to bring fear, but remember, he can only roar like a lion; he is not a lion! He can only act like he's taking our children, act like our sickness is unto death, act like he has the power to make us lose our minds. Satan can't touch us! We are God's children! Because Jesus Christ died for our sins, God excludes us from eternal damnation and every plot and scheme of Satan that he has devised here on earth for our demise.

Furthermore, 1 Peter 2:9 states *But you are a chosen generation, a royal priesthood, a holy nation, His own special people, that you may proclaim the praises of Him who called you out of darkness into His marvelous light.* As Christians, the Royal Family of Jesus Christ is our new birthright. We are heirs of God and joint-heirs with Jesus Christ, meaning we have All-Inclusive Kingdom Benefits and direct access to God our Father!

Day 14: A Time of Reflection and Renewal

Have I ever had an experience of being excluded and it turned out to be a good thing? _____

_____

_____

Have I ever relied on God's guidance, rather than worrying about an outcome?_____

_____

_____

How am I protected from Satan, the evil one?_____

_____

_____

_____

Are there people, friends or family, who I could help by including them in my faith?_____

_____

_____

_____

DAY 15

I Need An Understanding

Lindsey, an eleventh-grade student, struggled all school year in her math class. She did not fully understand some of the math equations, so she found it challenging to study. During the school year, her teacher offered her tutoring several times, but Lindsey chose cheerleading over going to tutoring. She took her final exam and did not pass. This exam determined whether she would pass the class. Consequently, Lindsey failed and had to repeat math during her senior year. Lindsey's parents informed her that she could not participate in cheerleading the next school year since she needed to receive tutoring in math, which was a course she had to pass to graduate from high school.

Lindsey's senior year started, and she was ready to knock this math class out of the ballpark. She attended tutoring sessions, and her grades improved tremendously. By the end of the school year, she was helping other students who were struggling. Lindsey passed her midterm math exam with a B grade. Although she passed her midterm, she remained committed to her tutoring. Her peers frequently asked her about getting back on the cheerleading team, but Lindsey was determined not to fail this time around. As finals approached, she developed a study group who looked up to Lindsey, not only because she was a senior, but because she had taken the class before, failed it, and came back as a shining star in the class. Lindsey and her study group passed their finals. Lindsey passed with an A and passed the math class with an A this time around. The problem wasn't that Lindsey couldn't pass the math class before, but she had her priorities in the wrong place. Lindsey felt she could prioritize cheerleading before an area that needed more of her time and attention, where she needed more understanding. She got caught up in the hype of cheerleading and neglected what was essential and crucial to her success at that time.

As with Linda's experience, there are areas in our lives where we notice we are failing or lacking an understanding, but we choose to neglect this area or issue in our lives. We decide to wear a mask and pretend that everything is fine, which causes us to get stuck and find ourselves in a place of misery. God will then require us to repeat the process, so we learn from it, grow and move forward in the things of Him and into our destiny. Proverbs 4:7 states, *Wisdom is the principal thing; Therefore get wisdom. And in all your getting, get understanding.* When going on our life journey, we certainly need wisdom, and we must get an understanding. We may know what to do but not know how to do it or what is required to get it done. We must assess: what does God want me to learn? What is His purpose for where I am right now? Am I walking in God's perfect will for my life or His permissive will? How does this help me to grow my relationship with God? How does this affect my success and destiny? How can I help others?

When Lindsey repeated her process, she was able to help others along the way. We cannot lead others where we have not gone. People want to know that you have overcome obstacles and made it through successfully, that you learned from your failures and came out a winner! You cannot learn without understanding what went wrong. Don't be moved by what you see others doing because you won't understand their process.

Day 15: A Time of Reflection and Renewal

What is one takeaway that I have from today's reading?

_____

_____

_____

Is there an area of my life that I am neglecting to give needed time and attention? _____

_____

_____

Is there an area of my life where I have failed in the past and can I correct it? _____

_____

_____

Do I clearly understand where I am and where I am going?

_____

_____

_____

DAY 16

Are You Fully Protected?

Have you ever gone through seasons in your life where you have had a series of unfortunate events? If I were to equate it to familiar seasons, I might call it a "Hurricane Season." It's a time where you've made great preparations to endure some possible natural disasters. Your home is full of supplies (generator, water, batteries, portable radio, flashlights, non-perishable items, etc.), and you have hurricane-impact windows. The natural disaster hits, then another and another merely weeks apart. You notice your roof is now leaking, causing significant damages. In preparation for hurricane season, you failed to have the home properly inspected. You also realized that your homeowners insurance was canceled months prior, which occurred with many residents, especially in Florida.

Just like in the natural, so it is in the Spirit. You wonder why you are always on the losing end. We must ensure that we are covered spiritually at all times. The Word of God tells us in Ephesians 7:12-17, *For we do not wrestle against flesh and blood, but against principalities, against powers, against the rulers of the darkness of this age, against spiritual hosts of wickedness in the heavenly places. Therefore, take up the whole armor of God that you may be able to withstand in the evil day, and having done all, to stand. Stand therefore, having girded your waist with truth, having put on the breastplate of righteousness, and having shod your feet with the preparation of the gospel of peace; above all, taking the shield of faith with which you will be able to quench all the fiery darts of the wicked one. And take the helmet of salvation, and the sword of the Spirit, which is the word of God.*

Just like we need to fully assess our physical properties for possible risk and ensure we have insurance to cover damages and losses, we must do the same in the Spirit. We do not need a meteorologist to let us know that a hurricane is on its way. God has already let us know that we must be girded in the Spirit. It doesn't matter if you're saved, sanctified, filled with the Holy Ghost, have money, prestige, good health, and own your own business. If you do not wear the Armor of God at all times, you are not fully protected.

Notice the scenario of someone having all the supplies, but who did not correctly assess their home and insurance to ensure full protection. All it takes is a crack for the enemy to get in and destroy you and your family. Just like one small crack in a roof can cause significant damages to a home and personal property inside the house, that is how Satan seeks to devour God's people. He wants to catch you with your guard down. He wants to sneak in your life. He takes advantage of the minuscule areas that you leave open.

I encourage you to do a thorough assessment of your life today. Do you consistently gird yourself with the whole Armor of God? Do you get tired and put your weapons down? God always has your back, but you must accept Jesus Christ into your heart and as your Lord and Savior. However, spiritual warfare is constant, and you must ensure that you are fully protected.

Day 16: A Time of Reflection and Renewal

Am I always prepared and ready for a spiritual storm?

_____

_____

_____

How can I keep myself prayed up and confident in God?

_____

_____

_____

After my reading today, what practical steps can I take to be ready for whatever comes my way?_____

_____

_____

_____

How can I impart my knowledge of spiritual protection to others?_____

_____

_____

DAY 17

It's Me I See

Rachel is a female physical therapist in her mid-thirties, single, with no children. Rachel became accustomed to traveling to see family and friends whenever she wanted. However, this past year has been extremely difficult for her due to the pandemic's social distancing laws. She received a furlough, putting her out of work for months. Rachel noticed that she began changing drastically in her features, behaviors, and attitude and no longer felt like herself. Looking in the mirror had become a part of her daily routine as she took extra careful attention to her appearance.

Rachel started eating and sleeping a lot. She began gaining weight rather quickly and would look in the mirror and make negative comments about herself. Whenever Rachel's friends tried to reach out to her virtually, she always gave them an excuse. Whenever Rachel communicated with anyone, she was short, rude, and made negative comments about herself and others. Rachel's family and friends never witnessed this behavior. Rachel began sabotaging herself and comparing herself to others who were married and had children. Her daily visits to the mirror became a time to put herself down.

After not reaching Rachel for several weeks, her mother came over to Rachel's home, telling her to snap out of it.

Rachel's mother said to her that she was not herself. She listed for Rachel all of the positive characteristics, beauty, and talents she possessed and her accomplishments with her education and owning her home. Rachel burst into tears and said she is tired of being someone she is not. She told her mother that she was everything her mother and father wanted her to be but not who she wanted to be. She said her parents forced her to be skinny, have short hair, and have friends they chose. She looked in the mirror and said, "Who I See Is Me." She said, I'm plump, my hair is long, I have pimples, and I'm not as nice as you all want me to be. Rachel felt forced to pretend that her life was perfect in others' eyes to please her mother and father. Rachel was ready to be who she was. Rachel told her mother that becoming an astronaut was her dream that both her mother and father had crushed.

Rachel insisted she was now changing her career. She had often been afraid to bring guys to her parents' house because she was afraid they would disapprove. Rachel decided she would date whomever she wanted to date and wouldn't introduce any man to her parents. Her mother sobbed and denied the allegations. Although Rachel's attitude was negative towards herself and others, she continued to look in the mirror and sort through some internal issues which caused her behaviors; This was a breakthrough for Rachel. Over the next five years, Rachel got married, had a baby, and pursued her dreams of becoming an Astronaut. She also made friends with diverse groups of people.

Are you your authentic you? Are you trying to please someone else? Do you find yourself tired of the image you see in the mirror? No matter what others want for you, know that God has made you who you are, and you do not have to change that for anyone. Whether you feel good or bad, big or small, tall or short, educated or uneducated, you were fearfully and wonderfully made by God (Psalm 139:14). I encourage you to embrace the person God has made. He has put desires into your heart that align with your God-given purpose and destiny. Jeremiah 29:11 states *For I know the thoughts that I think toward you says the Lord, thoughts of peace and not of evil, to give you a future and a hope.*

Although parents want the best for their children, God determined their destiny before birth. Parents make mistakes, but God does not. I encourage you to seek God for His will for your life and be the fulfilled individual God uniquely intended you to be. When we are not our authentic selves, we will become restless, angry, and frustrated.

Day 17: A Time of Reflection and Renewal

Who is it I see when I look in the mirror?_____

_____

_____

_____

What aspects of who I am were created to please others?

_____

_____

_____

What practical steps can I take to find my authentic self?

_____

_____

_____

How will pursuing my own personal dreams impact my life?

_____

_____

_____

DAY 18

What Are Your Vital Signs?

Our neighbor, Mr. John, was rushed to the emergency room for having trouble breathing. When the paramedics arrived at his home, the first thing they checked was his vital signs. His blood pressure was high, and his oxygen level was low. They immediately put an oxygen mask on his face and started an I.V. with fluids. However, when he arrived at the hospital, he went into cardiac arrest; they were losing him, he was suffering a heart attack. One nurse kept her eyes on his vitals as the other nurses and doctors worked on Mr. Jones. He had to be revived twice but made it. Mr. Jones had to have emergency surgery to perform a quadruple bypass, but he made it through. He had a list of lifestyle changes related to his health and strict instructions to stay alive.

Mr. John did not believe in going to the doctor. He had not been in twenty years. As this occurred with Mr. John physically, this can also happen with you spiritually. When was the last time you had a spiritual check-up? What are your spiritual vital signs? According to the Merriam Webster Dictionary, vital signs are the pulse rate, respiratory rate, body temperature, and blood pressure. Another definition is ". . . measurable variables considered to indicate the general state or condition of something." Vital signs depict whether you are living or not, whether you are healthy or not. Consistent check-ups are necessary.

To check your vital signs in the Spirit would require you to assess your prayer life (communication with God) and your relationship with Jesus Christ. Have you accepted him as your Lord and Savior as stated in Romans 10:9? Is your faith in the Almighty God? Hebrews 11:6 states, *But without faith, it is impossible to please Him, for he who comes to God must believe that He is and that He is a rewarder of those who diligently seek Him.* Do you read your Bible? Joshua 1:8 states, *This book of the law shall not depart out of your mouth; but you shall meditate therein day and night, that you may observe to do according to all that is written therein: for then you shall make your way prosperous, and then you shall have good success.*

If you are missing any one of these spiritual tools vital to the life and success as a Christian, you may want to do an assessment and re-evaluate how you've been surviving. Are you weary and feel like giving up? Do you lack peace? Do you lack joy? Are you up today and down tomorrow? Are you burdened financially? Do you have unhealthy relationships? Do you question God's voice? Do you trust God only when things are good? If you've answered yes to any of these questions, your vital signs are unstable, and you are susceptible to face cardiac arrest in the Spirit. The devil is about to devour you! Wake up! *Be sober; be vigilant, because your adversary the devil walks about like a roaring lion, seeking whom he may devour* (1 Peter

5:8). You cannot win in this Christian walk without knowing if you're spiritually healthy.

Day 18: A Time of Reflection and Renewal

What is one takeaway that I have from today's reading?

_____

_____

_____

Is there a specific area of my life where I am not taking my spiritual vitals? _____

_____

_____

Can I find time and space each day to read one Bible verse?

_____

_____

_____

Are my spiritual vital signs evident enough to impact others in a positive manner?_____

_____

_____

_____

DAY 19

Follow The Light

Shirley found out that her grandmother, who raised her, was terminally ill. Her grandmother lived in Georgia, which was over 400 miles away. Shirley had to make a quick decision to go to her but had no one who could travel with her. She had a friend check the tires on her vehicle, and he deemed it safe for her to go.

During her travel, she often encountered some very dark roads. She depended on the bright lights on her car. She spoke with several people before leaving home, who advised her to keep her eyes on the road and follow the light. Shirley ran into bad weather conditions—a tropical storm. She began to feel nervous and anxious as the rain poured down, the winds blew, and thunder and lightning struck across the skies. Tracy realized she still had a few more hours to go. Shirley ensured she sat straight up in her seat and followed the light. At one point, Shirley wanted to pull over but did not think that would be safe as she was traveling alone, and stopping would cause her to draw attention to her car. Shirley looked at her cell phone and noticed that it had no service. She kept her focus on the road ahead, and the only way to do so was via the lights from her vehicle. Shirley began to pray and ask God to help her arrive safely, without any mechanical problems. Shirley had been traveling for six hours when she noticed that the light became dim; one of her headlights went out. Shirley now had only one light that could help guide her. She had to trust God that the other light would not go out, but Shirley felt a sense of peace, knowing that God had her back. After traveling another hour and forty-five minutes, she saw more and more lights on each side of her illuminating from the homes.

Shirley felt a sense of relief as she realized that she was entering her grandmother's country town. She thanked God for even illuminating the one headlight that held up for her to get there. Shirley arrived safe and sound.

Have you ever felt like you didn't know where you were going in life because everything appeared dark and bleak? Have you ever had a storm in darkness? Were you ever afraid, feeling alone, and losing hope, peace, and direction? Although Shirley was traveling by herself and driving in poor weather conditions, she realized that she had a light to follow, and although one went out, it was enough to help her with where she needed to go. Most importantly, Shirley knew that the ultimate light would protect her! John 8:12 states: *Then Jesus spoke to them again, saying, I am the light of the world. He who follows Me shall not walk in darkness but have the light of life.*

God shines His light for us during our darkest moments. God's light represents hope, peace, salvation, deliverance, healing, and life.

When you believe that Jesus Christ died for your sins, that He was buried and has risen, you no longer live in darkness but His marvelous light. Isaiah 9:2 gives us a prophecy about what was to occur when Jesus would come. *The people who walked in darkness have seen a great light; those who dwelt in the land of the shadow of death, upon them a light has shined.* Darkness represents death, and light represents life. With Jesus, there is life, and life abundantly! There is everlasting life in Jesus Christ. *For God so loved the world that He gave His only begotten Son that whosoever believes on Him shall not perish but have everlasting life* (John 3:16).

Amid the chaos, uncertainty, crisis, a fallen economy, social unrest, and an unprecedented severe health pandemic, I encourage you to keep your eyes fixed on Jesus! Psalm 27:1 states, *The Lord is my light and my salvation; whom shall I fear? The Lord is the strength of my life; of whom shall I be afraid?* The devil's job is to make you have doubt and fear based on what you see and hear. He knows when you walk in the light; you can see him for who he is: someone with trickery, schemes, plots, wicked devices, and more.

When you follow Jesus, His light will lead you to unlock mysteries, dreams, visions, prophecies, and destiny. His light will guide your children out of the darkness. His light will change the heart of Kings in your favor, and His light will open doors for you that no man can shut! Your life depends on following the light, which is in Christ Jesus.

Day 19: A Time of Reflection and Renewal

Was there ever a time in my life when I was alone but sensed God's presence helping me? _____

_____

_____

Where is the spiritual light in my life? _____

_____

_____

How can I stay in God's light? What continual steps can I take?

_____

_____

_____

_____

What impact will this have on me, my family and others?

_____

_____

_____

_____

DAY 20

This Is The Day

We often quote this well-known scripture written by King David; *This is the day that the Lord has made, we will rejoice and be glad in it* (Psalm 118:24). The amplified version states, *This [day in which God has saved me] is the day which the LORD has made; Let us rejoice and be glad in it.* This scripture refers to the day of salvation. The same Jesus, the stone which the builders rejected, became the Chief Cornerstone. God already had a greater plan for Him. He elevated Jesus to be seated at the right hand of Him! If it were not for Jesus dying for our sins, our days would be dark and hopeless! What a reason to rejoice!!

This is the day that we should remind ourselves of God's Grace and Mercy. Let us rejoice and be glad! Each day, God gives us new mercies (Lamentations 3:22-23). Even after Jesus saved our souls from the penalty of sin (eternal damnation), God grants us the continued mercy we need when we fall short, when we don't obey His voice, when we commit sins of omission or commission, when we fall short of His glory.

This is the day that God has given to us as a new opportunity to spread the Gospel of Jesus Christ. 2 Corinthians 5:18-19 states, *Now all things are of God, who has reconciled us to Himself through Jesus Christ, and has given us the ministry of reconciliation*. As believers in Jesus Christ, we should rejoice that God has chosen us to share what Christ has done on the cross, not only for us, but for all unbelievers, realizing that we were once sinners, but we are saved by grace through faith. Believers should not just know this for themselves but look for an opportunity to share this with an unbeliever. Let us rejoice and be glad!

This is the day that God has made for us to spread the love of Jesus Christ. John 13:34-35 states, *A new commandment I give to you, that you love one another; as I have loved you, that you also love one another. By this, all will know that you are My disciples if you have love for one another.* We must love, even when we feel like others do not deserve our love. We did not deserve God's love for us, to the extent that He gave His only begotten son to die for our sins that we should not perish but have everlasting life (John 3:16). God gives us a new day to embrace this fact. Let us rejoice and be glad!

Finally, this is the day that we must walk in faith. Hebrews 11:6 states, *But without faith, it is impossible to please Him, for he who comes to God must believe that He is and that He is a rewarder of those who diligently seek Him.* God has and continues to prove His love to us. He provides for our family and us; He protects our family and us. He gives us our needs and most of our wants and desires. God makes ways out of no ways for us. He has given us jobs, houses, cars, health, and wealth.

God blesses and promises us that our seed shall be blessed. Who wouldn't trust a God like Jehovah God?

Today is a New Day, a new season, and God is doing a New Thing! Will you trust Him to know that He has you and the entire world in His hand? Let us remember that our day is full of reasons why we should rejoice and be glad in our joy.

Day 20: A Time of Reflection and Renewal

What are the blessings I can list that God has bestowed on me and my family? _____

_____

_____

Do I rejoice daily in God's love for me, His gifts and grace?

_____

_____

_____

What are practical steps I can take to realize God's love for me and feel joy in it? _____

_____

_____

_____

How could my joy impact my family and others? _____

_____

_____

_____

DAY 21

I Hear The Sound

Jaiden, my four-year-old grandson (little drummer boy), literally came into this world with the ability to hear a particular sound that would prompt him to move and strike up a beat. When his mother was pregnant, she played music to him, and his favorite song in the womb was "Put A Praise On It" by Tasha Cobbs. He would move about in her belly each time this song was on. When Jaiden was born, he heard the sound of this song and was alert and attentive. By the time Jaiden was six months, he would bounce up and down in the cutest little bouncer, similar to a baby's walker, without the wheels. There was a song someone made up for him, and as they clapped and sang, he would bounce and bounce. He would stop each time they stopped, then start up again when they would start up again; he would wait for the sound. It was not only cute and funny but astounding to see how this six-month-old baby was so attentive and on-beat with music and sounds. Jaiden was making beats with his mouth at age one and used anything that he could to beat to the sound of gospel music. Jaiden could hear music and had the right timing when he went along with the beat. Anyone who knows music can relate to this. Jaiden is now on his second drum set, and #2 is a real drum set. No doubt, he will go on to be a great drummer. It all started because he was able to hear a particular sound.

God has a sound on the spiritual airwaves that He expects His people to hear and listen to, so they will know He is there, He is speaking, and understand when He gives directions and directives. Ezekiel gave many examples of hearing sounds, which represented the presence of God and His manifestations, as Ezekiel, the Prophet, had a great call to the rebellious children of Israel. Ezekiel 3:10-14 states, *Moreover He said to me: Son of man, receive into your heart all My words that I speak to you, and hear with your ears. And go, get to the captives, to the children of your people, and speak to them and tell them, Thus says the Lord God, whether they hear, or whether they refuse. Then the Spirit lifted me up, and I heard a great rumbling sound behind me, blessed be the glory of the Lord in His place. I also heard the noise of the wings of the living creatures that touched one another, and the noise of the wheels beside them, and a great thunderous noise. So the Spirit lifted me up and took me away, and I went in bitterness, in the heat of my spirit; but the hand of the Lord was strong upon me.*

Ezekiel did not want to deal with Israel's hard-hearted people, but God gave him that assignment and gave him specific instructions. Ezekiel was in sync with God; He knew His sound. Ezekiel 37:7 states, *So I prophesied as I was commanded; and as I prophesied, there was a noise, and behold, a rattling; and the bones came together, bone to its bone.* This scripture is a prophetic portrayal of the rebirth of Israel. God was faithful to Israel and restored its people.

God is still faithful today. In tumult and confusion, God has a more excellent sound. He has a sound of deliverance, a sound of freedom, a sound of restoration, and victory. There is a sound that requires you to be in sync with God. God is doing a new thing, and He has given you the assignment to carry out His plan. However, you cannot hear the sound if you are distracted. You cannot hear the sound if you are walking in fear, and you cannot hear the sound if you are complacent. I encourage you today to quiet yourself, clear out the clutter in your mind, and renew your mind, so you can be like Jaiden and follow the beat. Be like Ezekiel, and move or shift with the sound.

Day 21: A Time of Reflection and Renewal

What is one takeaway that I have from today's reading?

_____

_____

_____

Where in my life have I closed off God's sound? _____

_____

_____

_____

How can I better discern God's sound? _____

_____

_____

_____

What impact will following God's sound have on my life, my family and others? _____

_____

_____

DAY 22

It's Not About Me

Samantha was an only child, raised with her mother and father. She wanted for nothing as she had everything she wanted. She wore the best clothes and shoes at her school, yet she was a very humble child. Samantha's parents taught her the principle of giving, "Give and it will be given unto to you," at an early age. Samantha chose a classmate each school year for her parents to "adopt a child," as in choosing a child to bless. Samantha began this when she started second grade and continued through her senior year of high school. Samantha's parents had the approval of the principal and school district. They ensured that the students and their parents never knew who was blessing them as they did not want to put Samantha in an awkward position with the student and her other peers. They bought school supplies, school uniforms and provided the funds for field trips, book fairs, and whatever else was involved.

What Samantha liked most about this was the fact that she chose a new student each year. She observed the student for a month and told her parents who did not have school supplies, who did not have lunch money, and who appeared not to have been as fortunate as she was. Samantha was always on target with her choice of students. She also shared with others and realized that life was not about her but about helping others. Samantha assisted her peers with homework and became a tutor, which also became her part-time job. She took some of her money to help her parents bless the children, not that they needed her money. Samantha and her family were truly blessed. They all rejoiced when Samantha received a full academic scholarship for college and continued to bless others, joining a missionary team. She now travels abroad as a missionary.

What are you doing with your time and your resources? The Bible speaks this way, *Let nothing be done through selfish ambition or conceit, but in lowliness of mind let each esteem others better than himself* (Philippians 2:3). God blesses us with health, education, and wealth to give our time and resources to others. We may not be in a financial position like Samantha's parents, but we can be the vehicle like Samantha was to bless others. Samantha could have been selfish as an only child who lacked nothing but thanks to God that she had her parents who taught her biblical principles of giving and preferring others above herself. Your trials and your test are not about you. Your experiences (good or bad) are not about you. We are here to give others hope, especially if we have endured hardships and now are overcomers. We are not here to keep our mouths closed or wear a mask as if we have always lived the life of an angel. Someone needs to hear that you went through some of the same struggles they are currently going through, and you made it through, and you are now on the other side as a Victor! Not a Victim but a Victor! We are not here to keep our fist closed. A closed fist cannot receive anything. Luke 6:38 states, *Give, and it will be given to you: good measure, pressed down, shaken together, and running over will be put into your bosom. For with the same measure that you use, it will be measured back to you.*

Today, I encourage you to stop despising where you are if you are in an uncomfortable or difficult place. Someone told me during some of my darkest days that "it won't always be this way," and she was correct. Our trials come to make us strong. We are to be strong for others who are weak. James 1:27 states, *Pure and undefiled religion before God and the Father is this: to visit orphans and widows in their trouble and to keep oneself unspotted from the world.* Matthew 25:35-40 states, *For I was hungry, and you gave Me food; I was thirsty, and you gave Me drink; I was a stranger, and you took Me in; I was naked, and you clothed Me; I was sick, and you visited Me; I was in prison, and you came to Me. Then the righteous will answer Him, saying, 'Lord, when did we see You hungry and feed You, or thirsty and give You drink? When did we see You a stranger and take You in, or naked and clothe You? Or when did we see You sick, or in prison, and come to You? And the King will answer and say to them, Assuredly, I say to you, inasmuch as you did it to one of the least of these my brethren, you did it to me.*

Repeat it: **It Is Not About Me!** I encourage you to get over yourself and think about someone else. Help others while you are alive and well. Sacrifice a little. Can you stand to be blessed? Put purpose in your heart to be a blessing!

Day 22: A Time of Reflection and Renewal

Am I able to say "It's not about me"? _____

_____

_____

_____

How does giving to others affect me spiritually and emotionally? _____

_____

_____

Is there someone in my life right now I can help? _____

_____

_____

_____

What will be the impact of my generosity, either in service or in gifts to others? _____

_____

_____

_____

DAY 23

It Is Good To Praise

At nine years old, Little Jasmine came home from school with her report card and showed her mother and father. They both reviewed it and noticed that Jasmine not only made the honor roll, but she made all A's, making the Principal's Honor Roll. Jasmine's mother grabbed her and gave her big hugs and kisses, while her father gave her a thumbs-up and proceeded to continue watching sports. Jasmine was happy that her mother was so excited but felt second to the football game because her dad showed no interest in her accomplishment.

The very next day, her dad's car broke down. He worked on it for hours and could not fix it. Jasmine noticed how down her dad was. She crawled up in his arms and began to tell him how good of a dad he was, how he was her hero. Jasmine even insisted that he was the best dad of any of her friends' dads. Her dad told her to think of what she wanted as a reward for making all A's. She quickly said to him that she wanted money. When Jasmine came home from school the next day, her dad had put a card on her bed with $50 inside. Jasmine was the happiest little girl ever, but she did not realize that she made her dad feel on top of the world with her praise.

One week later, Gail went to work, and her husband's supervisor called to tell her that her husband had an accident at work, hurt himself, and was on his way to the emergency room. When she arrived, she walked into the room, and her husband, while in much pain, was giving God praise. What she soon realized was that he was praising God for his co-worker being alive. He explained to Gail that he could have avoided his accident, but he jumped in to prevent his co-worker from taking a 20 ft. fall, then fell back and tripped, hurting his knees. However, his decision resulted in a need for knee surgery and staying out of work for two months on worker's compensation, losing a good portion of his check. It also required Gail to take time off to care for him. Gail immediately praised her husband for saving someone else's life. She did not worry about the bills or anything else. Needless to say, his co-worker, who almost took the fall, was very grateful and went to the hospital with the supervisor, who also showed a lot of concern.

After his surgery, he woke up to a room full of flowers and balloons which read *Thank You-You're My Hero*, and cards with money inside. In addition to that, his colleagues from work took up a donation for him, raising $2500. Gail and her husband were blessed beyond measures as money continued to flow in for them.

It is good to give praise. Just like Jasmine's parents praised her for a job well done, we must praise God every day for His goodness. He blesses us each day with many blessings, seen and unseen. He not only gives us life, health and strength, but he has prevented us from taking a fall which would have ultimately resulted in a physical and spiritual death!

Gail's husband could have been selfish, but he decided to think of his coworker before thinking of himself. Gail could have reacted selfishly and scolded her husband for putting someone else before himself. However, she shared in his gratitude for being used by God to save his co-worker's life. Gail praised him for his bravery and praised God with him. Neither of them worried about the next moment or the next day, but they praised God for the very moment. In return, God blessed them beyond their imagination. One songwriter wrote the famous phrase, "When praises go up, blessings come down."

King David said in Psalm 22:3, *But thou art holy, O thou that inhabits the praises of Israel.* What this means is when Israel praised God, He came and dwelled among them. When we praise God in the good times and the bad times (it doesn't matter), He comes down from His throne and dwells among us in the spirit.

Jasmine's daddy asked her what she wanted after receiving her praise. What do you think our Daddy God is saying to us when we praise Him? If God takes the time to dwell in our midst as we give Him praise, He will not leave without blessing us. It may not manifest the same day, but you best believe He has already done it! What I like most is that Jasmine's praise for her daddy was unconditional. She praised him because of who she felt he was to her.

God is worthy of our praise! He does not have to do anything else for us! He gave His only Son to die for our sins so that we can be in the right relationship with Him, thereby having everlasting life! I do not need to go down the list of all God has done. I encourage you to find praise in your heart. Psalm 150:6 states, *Let everything that has breath praise the Lord. Praise the Lord!* Now it's time to reflect on the goodness of God and everything He has done for you. Take a praise break and give him a shout of praise with a loud voice!

Day 23: A Time of Reflection and Renewal

When was the last time I praised God for his many blessings?

_____

_____

_____

Is there someone whom I could make feel better by praising him or her?_____

_____

_____

When something in my life is troubling me, can I switch my focus to praise for something that is a gift from God?

_____

_____

_____

How can I be a role model for praising God and influence others to do the same? _____

_____

_____

DAY 24

Why Not You?

Growing up as a child with many allergies who lived off of water and calcium drops for the first two years of my life set me apart from my sister and cousins. They could practically eat whatever they wanted without worrying about unattractive breakouts, many doctor visits, medications, and sleepless nights, due to the constant skin irritation. I often wondered—why me? Experiencing the traumas of molestation, rape, physical, verbal and mental abuse, rejection, and abandonment as a child, I had often asked God—why me? Looking for love in all the wrong places, teenage pregnancy, teenage marriage, facing homelessness, evictions, car repossessions, failed relationships, and living the single parent life, I found myself asking God again—why me?

Finally, after surrendering my life to God, accepting my call to ministry, walking in my calling, married, pursuing my education, settling in my career, being a good (not perfect) mommy to my children, things began to look up for me. Did I say I surrendered my life to God? Oh yes, that's what I said. Then boom, I asked myself, what have I gotten myself into now? Chaos, drama, infidelity, rejection, all over again—abandonment all over again! This time I did not even think to ask God, why me because He beat me to it by saying, "Why Not You?"

I heard the voice of the Lord say, *I know the plans I think toward you, plans to prosper you and never harm you, to give you hope and a future* (Jeremiah 29:11). I knew that my future would look much brighter than my past. I knew that there was nothing impossible with God because, with Him, all things are possible. God told me that I would impact many lives worldwide through my testimony, and whatever negative experiences the enemy meant for my bad, He had already turned around for my good!

I know many of you have wondered why you are experiencing adversity that never seems to end. You have asked God the "why" question as well. You may feel life is unfair, and others appear to be better off than you. Well, they may be asking God the same question. I encourage you today to surrender everything, just like I did, and trust God with your heart and soul. Job said it this way, *But He knows the way that I take; when He has tested me, I shall come forth as gold* (Job 23:10). God will turn your mourning into dancing. He will turn your sorrow into joy. However, you must go through the process; the refiner's fire. Why you? The answer is, God has chosen you. What you have been through should have destroyed you, but it made you stronger! Now you can help someone else come out of the very same situation.

Day 24: A Time of Reflection and Renewal

Can I surrender everything to God and trust Him for all my good?_____

_____

_____

Am I ready to release the habits of negative thoughts?

_____

_____

_____

What would be the impact of me listing all that is not good in my life and surrendering each complaint to God? _____

_____

_____

_____

When I realize God's presence in my life, can I encourage others to do so as well? _____

_____

_____

DAY 25

I Finally Said Yes

Stacey and Robert, a beautiful couple, shared with a group at a couples' retreat about how they met and started dating. Robert said they both worked in the same building but for different companies. However, they would somehow see each other every day in the café. Was this intentional? Well, let's see. Robert explains how he would look at the clock every day and make sure he avails himself to leave on time to see Stacey. Robert said Stacey made his heart pound each time he saw her. After a couple of months of this, he said he finally offered to buy her lunch, but she humbly declined. Stacey chimed in and said she wanted to say yes but was being modest.

Another few weeks went by with them seeing each other, speaking, getting their lunch, and going back to work. One day Robert and Stacey saw each other in the parking garage. Her hands were full, so Robert offered to assist her, but she declined his assistance. The next day, Robert went to the café, but he did not see Stacey. You're talking about heart pounding and butterflies in the stomach; Robert said he felt like she avoided him and went at another time. Stacey said she got caught up on a call with a customer and skipped lunch; really, Stacey?

The next week, Robert said he planned it all out. He pre-paid for her lunch and was nowhere to be found in the café when she arrived. However, when she went to the elevator, he rushed to hold the elevator door open for her. Stacey said she blushed but proceeded back to work. Robert wrote his number on the container, and of course, the clerk at the cafe knew what was going on; she was undoubtedly in cahoots with him. Stacey opened the bag, saw the phone number on the container with his name, and a message asking her to "please call." Stacey was stunned, a little happy, she said, but she never called. Robert would not give up. He loved the challenge. He saw her a few days later and asked for her number, and she finally said yes!

Robert told the group he felt like screaming in the building, "She said yes!" However, it was not the time nor the place. Robert and Stacey talked over the phone and scheduled a date. Unfortunately, Stacey canceled their first date due to a family emergency. Robert waited patiently on Stacey. They scheduled another date a week later. They both said it was a night they will never forget. They laughed, danced and enjoyed each other. The dating continued for a year, and they got married. She said yes! They are five years strong and happily married.

How many times did God try to get your number, and you said no? How many times have you brushed him off? How many dates have you canceled with Him? It is typical and easy to run. It is easy to get stuck in your ways and put other concerns before Him.

God wants a yes from you today. The yes God wants from you is not out of convenience, *but I need You, Yes! I want You,*

Yes! I can't make it without You, Yes! I tried it on my own, but it's just doesn't work. Yes. God wants a yes. I said yes before, but it was not a for real, Yes! He wants a complete Yes, a Final Yes! When you give God a Yes, you will see your life change not just for the better, but for the best!

James 4:7 states, *Submit yourselves therefore to God. Resist the devil, and he will flee from you.* It doesn't mean that the devil will not continue to try you. Of course, he will! However, that does mean that you don't have to fight because *The battle does not belong to you, it belongs to the Lord* (2 Chronicles 2:15). God wants you to prosper and be healthy even as your soul prospers. God wants you to eat the good of the land which He has provided for you. His desire is for none to perish. God wants to give you your heart's desire, according to His will. I encourage you to say Yes to God. If you want a life of joy and peace, you want to say Yes to God! He is the solution to every problem and your answer to the mystery. He is peace where there is confusion, joy in sorrow, and hope for tomorrow.

Day 25: A Time of Reflection and Renewal

What is one takeaway that I have from today's reading?
_____
_____
_____

Have there been times God knocked on my door and I didn't answer? _____
_____
_____

After my reading today, what practical steps can I take for a more positive outcome? _____
_____
_____
_____

When have I heard a call from God and said yes to it? What happened as a result? _____
_____
_____

DAY 26

Walk By Faith

You may be thinking right now, walking by faith is easier said than done. The only difficult or frustrating part of walking by faith is walking in your own strength and might. Let me guess, some of you are absolutely over it! Well, I have good news for you today. You are exactly where God needs you to be; This is the place where you have done all that "you" know how to do, but still no change, no light at the end of the tunnel, no recourse. This situation reminds me of the familiar Bible passage about the woman with the issue of blood for twelve years. This woman spent all the money she had on physicians, with hopes that they had the proper medication to heal her disease. The Bible states that this woman heard that Jesus was passing by.

This woman could have allowed fear, doubt, and disbelief to cloud her thoughts. After all, she should have remained isolated due to her issue according to the laws during that time. However, she walked by faith, hoping no one would recognize her and punish her for breaking the laws during those times. The woman was desperate as she pressed her way through the crowd. She knew that if she could only touch Jesus, she would be made whole. She was able to touch the hem of the garment Jesus was wearing, and immediately, she was not only healed, but she was made whole. When the woman touched the hem of

His garment, Jesus felt the virtue leave His body, which supernaturally went into this woman. Jesus said to her, "Woman, your faith has made you whole," and instructed her to "go in peace" (Luke 8:43-48).

Would you like to have the peace of God that surpasses all understanding? Now is your opportunity to surrender all to God and trust Him to do the impossible. Trust God to lead and guide you. Trust God to open the doors that have been closed in your face. Trust God for the promotion. Trust God for a place to live for you and your family. Trust God to heal your body. Trust God for your child's and your entire family's deliverance. Trust God to provide for you. Trust God for your husband or wife. Trust God to heal your marriage. Trust God for change. Trust God to heal the land as you continue to pray. *Trust in the LORD with all your heart, and lean not on your own understanding; In all your ways acknowledge Him, and He shall direct your paths* (Proverbs 3:5-6).

Walking by faith is merely living a life surrendered to God. Because God is the Alpha and Omega (the beginning and the end), He wrote your life story. He knows the ways that you take. God said to Jeremiah and still says the same to you today, *For I know the thoughts that I think toward you, says the Lord, thoughts of peace and not of evil, to give you a future and a hope* (Jeremiah 29:11). When you walk by faith, and not by sight, you are confident that God has all that is ahead of you in His hand; He also has your back, for He is your rear guard.

Typically, when a person physically takes a walk, he or she knows what is ahead. Whenever people travel, especially in an unfamiliar place, they seek guidance (road maps and navigation systems) to reach their destination. We can deduce that we feel a sense of security when we are in the know. We can relax when we know where we are going, what the outcome will be, or what next step we need to take. However, God has created us not to rely on our limited selves wholly but solely on Him, who is limitless. He needs no assistance.

I encourage you today to walk by faith. Like the woman with the issue of blood, I implore you to reach out and touch the heart of Jesus. Our faith moves God. This woman showed Jesus just how desperate she was for Him. This journey does not have to be overwhelming. Yes, you will have some good days and some bad days, but your good days will always outweigh the bad! Hebrews 11:6 states, *But without faith, it is impossible to please Him, for he who comes to God must believe that He is and that He is a rewarder of those who diligently seek Him. You only need to trust God!*

God has taken us to a place of unfamiliarity to show the world that He is God; He is supreme! But He has promised never to leave or forsake you! Trust God all the way. He wants to blow your minds. He wants to give you exceedingly, abundantly, above all that you can ask or think. Sometimes, you cannot receive all that God has for you because you are too focused on what should be in God's hands. You have to give it to

Him and take it back and repeat this cycle over and over again. I encourage you to make a conscious effort to leave everything in God's hands and trust that He can and will handle it!

Day 26: A Time of Reflection and Renewal

What have I learned from the story of the woman with the issue of blood who touched the hem of Jesus' garment?

_____

_____

_____

What example does the story set for me? _____

_____

_____

Can I relinquish worry and reach out for Jesus' cloak?

_____

_____

_____

How might my life change if I was to consistently walk by faith?_____

_____

_____

_____

DAY 27

Telephone Disconnected?

As a little girl singing the song, "Jesus Can Work It Out" with my mother and sisters, my grandfather took great delight in our singing the part of the verse that says, "telephone disconnected, waiting for your next paycheck." The entire song gives examples of different struggles and testings, with its primary message: no matter what you are going through, Jesus Can and Will Work it Out.

As you face disappointment, obstacles, storms, trials, and tests, your spiritual phone may appear to be disconnected. In this case, you are not waiting on your next paycheck to reconnect your phone. In fact, money is not involved at all. You must wait until God speaks and answer your prayers. How hard is that? Who wants to wait for an answer? Who wants to feel ignored? I am so glad you asked!

Isaiah 40:31 states, *But those who wait on the Lord Shall renew their strength; They shall mount up with wings like eagles, They shall run and not be weary, They shall walk and not faint.* This passage of scripture tells us that we will not always receive an answer right away. God will have us wait, even though his answer is Yay and Amen! God wants to know that you will trust Him. God loves us so much that He does not need to operate like a fairy godfather in the world of fairy tales, who magically appears when you call His name! Most of the time, God has us waiting to produce character in us. We cannot grow and develop spiritually, personally or professionally, if we do not know how to wait on God. In the midst of you thinking the telephone is disconnected, God teaches you how to properly communicate with Him. He wants you to pray—talk to Him. He wants you to read and meditate on His Word; God speaks to us through His Word (the Bible). He wants you to rest in Him, knowing that He will always come through. He wants you to be steadfast and unmovable. He wants you to be strong enough to soar like an eagle. He wants you to be like a tree planted by the rivers so that you can withstand the rainy days, the hail pounding on the roof, and all the effects of the storms of life.

When the disciples were on the boat with Jesus, as Jesus fell asleep and the storms raged, they were immediately afraid and felt like Jesus did not care about their safety. I can only imagine them calling His name and not getting a response, only to find Him asleep. I am sure they had an overwhelming feeling of anxiety, as with some of you when you call on Him and feel He is not answering you. Jesus was in the boat's stern, but still near the disciples, just like He is there with you every second of each day. If the disciples had only trusted that they were friends of, and in the very presence of, the Miracle Worker, Jesus could have continued to rest, and their faith would have pulled them through the storm. Jesus had to get up, and rebuke the wind and say to the sea (waves), "Peace be still," and there was an immediate calm. Jesus had to address the disciple's lack of faith (Mark 4:35-41).

How many times has God had to pull you out of the very process that would have made you whole? How many times did He have to abruptly stop your promotion because you would not wait to hear from Him? How many times have you had to retake the test because you jumped ship when the storm began to rage? How many times did He have to tell you to wait so that he can build your character to keep you where He wants to take you? Rest assured, as long as you have accepted Jesus as your Lord and Savior, you can access Him directly. The veil was rent when Jesus died on the cross and rose again. He is the High Priest!

The only thing that separates us from God is sin. Jesus came to save the lost, to redeem you from the penalty of sin, which is death. *For the wages of sin is death but the gift of God is eternal life through Jesus Christ our Lord* (Romans 6:23). Not accepting Jesus as your Lord and Savior is a sure disconnect. I implore you to receive Him in your heart today. Romans 10:9 states that *if you confess with your mouth the Lord Jesus and believe in your heart that God has raised Him from the dead, you will be saved.*

Day 27: A Time of Reflection and Renewal

Am I able to wait when I ask for God's help? _____

_____

_____

_____

Was there a time I did wait and finally God answered me?

_____

_____

_____

Is there a place in my life right now where I am willing to wait for God to fix the problem? _____

_____

_____

_____

Do I ever feel disconnected when I communicate with God?

_____

_____

_____

DAY 28

Jesus Take The Wheel

Hats off to Songwriters Brett James, Hillary Lindsey, and Gordie Sampson of "Jesus Take the Wheel," recorded by Carrie Underwood in 2005. It has been a popular cliché since. While I love the lyrics to this song, which describes a lady in an emergency, as she drives her car, loses control, and asks Jesus to take the wheel, I must say that it is very typical for people to call on Jesus in an emergency. Yes, He is there for us to call upon during these times, but when we ask Jesus to take the wheel, it should not just be in times of distress, uncertainty, or an emergency. When your children are misbehaving— Jesus, take the wheel. When your marriage is on the rocks—Jesus, take the wheel. When your job is doing a massive layoff—Jesus, take the wheel. When you cannot be in control, then it is—Jesus, take the wheel. Yes, by all means, Jesus, please take the wheel during these difficult times.

However, when we declare that Jesus is Lord over our lives, He should already have the wheel. When we say that we trust Him with our lives, our family, health, jobs, finances, education, dreams, plans, future, and destiny, He should already have the wheel. When Jesus takes the wheel, that means He is in complete control. Oh my! "Control," there's that scary word. If it is not "you" in control, you feel inadequate, untrusting, develop anxiety and do whatever it takes to regain control. God wants you to say what you mean and mean what you say. Say it with me—"Jesus Take the Wheel."

Psalm 37:23-24 states, *The steps of a good man are ordered by the LORD, And He delights in his way. Though he falls, he shall not be utterly cast down; For the LORD upholds him with His hand.* This is Jesus taking the wheel. You please God when you allow Him to take the wheel. This scripture passage guarantees us that God will always keep you in His hands if you allow Him to have complete control over your life. He may lead you into the valley, but He's there. He may lead you up the mountain, but He's there. He may lead you in the forest, but He's there. He may lead you in the wilderness, but He's there. He may lead you in the storm, but He's there. The keyword here is "lead." Because Jesus is leading, He knows the way through and out. The only requirement is for you to follow Him. King David said: *He leads me beside the still waters. He restores my soul; He leads me in the paths of righteousness For His name's sake. Yea, though I walk through the valley of the shadow of death, I will fear no evil; For You are with me; Your rod and Your staff, they comfort me* (Psalm 23:2-4).

King David was a bonafide Shepherd Boy, who knew what it meant to lead the sheep because if he didn't, they would be lost. Being a Shepherd Boy gave King David a sense of appreciation for God, his Heavenly Father, being his Shepherd. Just as King David said, God will lead you exactly where it is necessary to go. He will lead you to a place of rest, refreshing, and restoration.

God will comfort you in your darkest hour and will correct you and redirect you when you don't listen or attempt to wander off.

God yearns and awaits that same relationship with you that King David had with Him. God is saying to you today, *Come to Me, all you who labor and are heavy laden, and I will give you rest. Take My yoke upon you and learn from Me, for I am gentle and lowly in heart, and you will find rest for your souls. For My yoke is easy, and My burden is light* (Matthew 11:28-30). Will you give God the wheel, and this time, remain the passenger? Where God wants to take you, you are incapable of carrying yourself. I like that song that goes, "Can't Nobody Do Me Like Jesus." I will say today, Can't Nobody Lead You Like Jesus! God wants to open doors for you that no man can shut. God wants to help you exceedingly, abundantly, above all you can ask or think. Will you trust God today?

Day 28: A Time of Reflection and Renewal

What is one takeaway that I have from today's reading?
_____

_____

_____

Although I may not have known it at the time, have I had an experience where Jesus did take the wheel for me?

_____

_____

_____

Where in my life right now would I like Jesus to take the wheel? _____

_____

_____

_____

How do I feel knowing that Jesus has or wants the wheel to my life?_____

_____

_____

DAY 29

Reset

I recall God speaking to me in March 2020, as I was making breakfast one morning. "I am getting ready to do a reset in you," He said. He then showed me in a vision how the test button is pushed in a bathroom when an electrical appliance will not come on and how pressing the reset button gives it power. I began to give God the praise for the Reset. I began to share it with others. Then I began to hear that word more and more. God was confirming His Word to me.

How does this reset button work? In a nutshell, there is usually a test and reset button inside your bathroom or any room near a sink, an electrical outlet covered by an electrical plate. The buttons are designed to pop-out if an electrical cord comes in contact with a certain amount of water to prevent shock. Usually, the homeowner or electrician presses the reset button after everything checks out fine; the power is available again. The homeowner or electrician checks the test and reset buttons at least semi-annually to ensure they work properly.

Let's look at this on the level of the Spirit. There is a series of tests God will allow us to go through, and just before an overload, God will do a reset. Just before we make a wrong move or a wrong turn, God will do a reset. When He sees that you have gone through trials, heartaches, pain, disappointments, or illnesses, but have proven to be faithful and withstood the misfortune, He will do a reset. Before you feel like you are about to throw in the towel, He will do a reset. Just before you go back and repeat a negative cycle in your life, God will step in and do a reset. 1 Corinthians 10:13 states, *No temptation has overtaken you except such as is common to man; but God is faithful, who will not allow you to be tempted beyond what you are able, but with the temptation will also make the way of escape, that you may be able to bear it.* We like to say it like this, "God will put no more on you than you can bear." God knows when it is time to reset His children. God gives us the power to endure. He provides us with the ability to run on.

When God did a reset in my life, my perspective changed, and I was more enlightened. When God reset me, my spiritual, emotional, and mental health enhanced. He also sharpened my discernment. God allowed me to go through the process of facing various difficult seasons, so when He reset me, I would be prepared to take the bold stance for what He had, and continues to have, in front of me.

Resetting involves rooting and grounding you. That physical reset button runs through wires that are "grounded." Jeremiah 17:8 states, For he shall be like a tree planted by the waters, which spreads out its roots by the river, And will not fear when heat comes; But its leaf will be green, And will not be anxious in the year of drought, Nor will cease from yielding fruit.

God is calling for His people to come forth so He can position them according to His plan. God wants to ensure that you are capable of standing and will not wither away in difficult and challenging times. God is waiting for your fruit to manifest for the hopeless, the lost, and the broken. Romans 8:19 states, *For the earnest expectation of the creation, eagerly waits for the revealing of the sons of God.* Are you ready to reset? When God presses the reset button, it's an automatic "Go" from there.

Day 29: A Time of Reflection and Renewal

Do I understand what a reset button is and does? _____

_____

_____

_____

Have I experienced a reset from God? _____

_____

_____

Is there a place in my life right now which I would like God to do a reset? _____

_____

_____

Do I know of someone else who may need a reset and how could I help him or her? _____

_____

_____

_____

DAY 30

Renew Your Mind

Former Head of the United Negro College Fund, Arthur Fletcher, coined the phrase, "A mind is a terrible thing to waste." As I thought about this phrase, I quickly thought of the plethora of information that enters our minds daily. Some of it we control, and some we do not. I could only deduce that the mind is similar to a computer database. It often gets overloaded, resulting in headaches, stress, anxiety, and fatigue. This overload can also affect our physical bodies, emotions, and spirit. If you are an individual who watches or listens to the news media or social media day in and day out, you probably would be a candidate not only for information overload but frustration, depression, anger, sorrow, you name it.

You must guard your eyes and your ear gates to preserve your mind. God has designed our minds to absorb what we put into them. However, there are times when information comes unexpectedly and is beyond our control. "Knowledge is Power," so you want to gain the essential and relevant information you need to succeed. There are also life experiences that will either stay in the forefront of your mind or your subconscious. The subconscious can have just as much or more significant effect on your behavior as the conscious mind. Why does the man who grew up in a violent home as a little boy struggle with alcohol addiction to numb the pain of replaying his father coming home drunk and abusing his mother every night of the week? Why does the woman who grew up in a volatile home, suffering verbal and physical abuse, attract men who verbally and physically abuse her? Why does the beautiful little girl who was rejected by her mother and father grow up looking for love in all the wrong places? Why does the child who people have told that she would never amount to anything settle for less? Why does the young lady experience teenage pregnancy after she was a victim of molestation and rape? Why are mental health issues at an all-time high? It is the power of the mind that can either make or break you. The good news is that you have a choice. However, everyone does not realize that they have the power to choose.

Joyce Meyer, an American Charismatic, Christian Author, Speaker, President of Joyce Meyer Ministries, and #1 New York Times bestselling author, published the all-time bestselling book, *Battlefield of the Mind*. This book deals with the different attacks on the mind (worry, doubt, confusion, depression, anger, and feelings of condemnation). It has helped so many people across the globe overcome these mind battles. What happens when you just cannot seem to clear your thoughts? You must decide what you will allow in your mind, which can ultimately get into your spirit. Your reactions towards others and particular issues are often based on what you have allowed to enter into your spirit man. It all starts with the mind. Most of the choices you make daily come from what you have going on in your mind. Some are good, and some can be detrimental not only to you but to your family members and friends.

Romans 12:2 states, *And do not be conformed to this world, but be transformed by the renewing of your mind, that you may prove what is that good and acceptable and perfect will of God.* It is easy to act like everyone else in the world, but if you are to be the disciples and followers of Jesus Christ, you must ensure that you renew your mind. Transformation cannot take place until you renew your mind. Have you wondered why you cannot progress towards the things of God and what He has destined for you? If you have not asked God to deliver your mind from old thinking, selfish thinking, doubtful thinking, and stinking thinking, you will continue to take one step forward and two steps backward.

Your mind must be clear and open to new ideas to get a fresh start. Nonsense may come, but you do not have to allow it to distract you. It does not have to take up space in your mind. If you desire a change, change what you allow to take up residence in your mind. Change may entail changing some of your company; it may mean changing some of your favorite shows or music. It does mean filling your mind with the Word of God so that you may be able to resist the devil when he comes. God will allow you to have your will or give you His perfect will, but again, He gives you a choice. Rest assured that only His perfect will is what will be good and acceptable to Him.

I encourage you to renew your mind today and every day. Ask God to declutter your mind from everything you have come in contact with daily that will not benefit you now or in the future. If it is not something that will add to your life, you do not need to entertain it. When you renew your mind, you will see old ways and bad habits drop off. You will be more attractive to people who are looking for hope and a better life. A renewed mind will give you more possibilities. It will improve your confidence, clarity of thought, and physical, emotional, and mental health.

Day 30: A Time of Reflection and Renewal

When I listen to my mind, what garbage do I find in there?

_____

_____

Is there a list of bad thoughts I can release and give to God?

_____

_____

_____

How can I practically take the time to be more discerning of my thoughts? _____

_____

_____

_____

What impact would emptying my mind of all negativity have on me and others? _____

_____

_____

DAY 31

Free

Free! Whew! Free is a small word with enormous and powerful meaning. According to Merriam-Webster's Dictionary, one definition of free is "not bound, confined, or detained by force." Whenever you feel that you cannot live your life according to God's will, you are bound in some form. If you have difficulty choosing between what is right or wrong, what is good for you or bad for you, what is moral or immoral, ethical or unethical, what is sinful or what is holy, then you are bound in some form. God gives us the freedom to choose. Although you have this freedom to choose, many are still bound mentally, emotionally, and spiritually.

You choose what clothes and shoes you will wear, what car you will drive, your home, your career path. You choose your boyfriend, girlfriend, husband, or wife. You choose your friends. You decide what food you will eat, how you want to spend your money, how you want to spend your time. You choose your religion or who you want to serve as your higher power. You select the time you go to bed and what time you want to wake up. Did you notice that I said what time you want to wake up? There are a few things you have no choice over, and they are your parents, your birthday, whether you will live to see the next second unless you choose to take your life (which I would not recommend), and your date of death. God remains in total control, even though He gives us the power to choose. With all the choices God allows, why do so many people get entangled in situations that keep them bound?

Being free is very simple. It starts with the power to choose. Like the different examples listed above, we can choose to be free with the choices we make. Freedom, however, starts in the mind. Once you have realized that circling the mountain over and over again will not change the scenery and that doing the same thing over and over again, expecting a different result is insanity, you may almost be ready to choose freedom. If you are in a place of oppression, something or someone has you bound. If you cannot make decisions on your own (without having some sort of disability or cognitive impairment), and you must poll the opinions of others to help you make simple decisions, you are bound. If you are unsure of yourself and battle with low self-esteem, you are bound. If you cannot love yourself and feel that you must be in a relationship to feel loved, you are bound. If you cannot be your authentic self, you are bound. If you live in misery, depression, anger, guilt, shame, jealousy, envy, or addiction, you are bound. If you are unstable, you are bound. If you are in an abusive (verbal, physical, emotional, sexual) relationship, you are bound. If you have a mental illness and you are non-compliant with your physician, psychiatrist, and counselor without having a medical reason, it is easy for you to become bound if you are not already.

Being free is a serious matter. Your very life depends on it. Your family and friends would greatly benefit from your freedom as well. Everyone and everything concerning you are at stake when you are bound. I strongly encourage you to pray and seek counseling to discover the root issue(s) of why you cannot break free so that you can get assistance to help you with the process of becoming delivered and set free.

Let me be very clear, if you have not accepted Jesus as your Lord and Savior, you are not spiritually free. However, the good news is that you can receive Him today. *If you would confess with your mouth that you are a sinner and believe in your heart that Jesus Christ died for your sins, was buried, and rose from the grave, you shall be saved* (Roman 10:9).

Even if you are a believer in Jesus Christ, you can still be bound if you have strongholds in your life. The bible states in John 8:30-36, *Then Jesus said to those Jews who believed Him, "If you abide in My word, you are My disciples indeed. And you shall know the truth, and the truth shall make you free." They answered Him, We are Abraham's descendants and have never been in bondage to anyone. How can You say, "You will be made free?" Jesus answered them, Most assuredly, I say to you, whoever commits sin is a slave of sin. And a slave does not abide in the house forever, but a son abides forever. Therefore if the Son makes you free, you shall be free indeed.* Galatians 5:1 states, "*Stand fast therefore in the liberty by which Christ has made us free, and do not be entangled again with a yoke of bondage.*

I am ecstatic to say that "I once was bound, but now I am free." Not only did God save my soul and deliver me from the penalty of sin (eternal damnation in hell), but God set me free from the torment of my past. God set me free from rejection and abandonment. God set me free from father and mother wounds. God set me free from low self-esteem. God set me free from feeling like I need a man to feel loved. God set me free from every generational cycle in my bloodline. God has set me free, and I say to you that it feels good to walk in liberty.

I encourage you to decree and declare that I am coming out today because I am now free! It is rewarding to be free. It is God's will for all of us to be free. When God sets you free, you have to remain free. I challenge you to continue to guard your freedom by renewing your mind daily and making the right choices. Above all, submit to God, resist the devil, and he will flee from you (James 4:7). I celebrate your freedom with you. Congratulations on your 31 Days of Renewal!

Day 31: A Time of Reflection and Renewal

Can you list the freedoms you have in your life? _____

_____

_____

_____

Are there areas in my life where I still feel spiritually and/or emotionally bound? If so, can I talk with a therapist, pastor or minister? _____

_____

_____

How can I set myself free through the Lord?_____

_____

_____

After working through these *31-Days of Renewal*, which practices are most valuable for me to cultivate?_____

_____

_____

_____

MY

31

DAILY

JOURNALS

DAY 1 JOURNAL

DAY 2 JOURNAL

DAY 3 JOURNAL

DAY 4 JOURNAL

DAY 5 JOURNAL

DAY 6 JOURNAL

DAY 7 JOURNAL

DAY 8 JOURNAL

DAY 9 JOURNAL

DAY 10 JOURNAL

DAY 11 JOURNAL

DAY 12 JOURNAL

DAY 13 JOURNAL

DAY 14 JOURNAL

DAY 15 JOURNAL

DAY 16 JOURNAL

DAY 17 JOURNAL

DAY 18 JOURNAL

DAY 19 JOURNAL

DAY 20 JOURNAL

DAY 21 JOURNAL

DAY 22 JOURNAL

DAY 23 JOURNAL

DAY 24 JOURNAL

DAY 25 JOURNAL

DAY 26 JOURNAL

DAY 27 JOURNAL

DAY 28 JOURNAL

DAY 29 JOURNAL

DAY 30 JOURNAL

DAY 31 JOURNAL

SCRIPTURAL REFLECTION

SCRIPTURAL REFLECTION

1. *The weapons we fight with are not the weapons of the world. On the contrary, they have divine power to demolish strongholds.* – 2 Corinthians 10:4

2. *Religion that God our Father accepts as pure and faultless is this: to look after orphans and widows in their distress and to keep oneself from being polluted by the world.* – James 1:27

3. *Submit yourselves, then, to God. Resist the devil, and he will flee from you.* – James 4:7

4. *Do not conform to the pattern of this world, but be transformed by the renewing of your mind. Then you will be able to test and approve what God's will is–his good, pleasing and perfect will.* – Romans 12:2

5. *These are the people who divide you, who follow mere natural instincts and do not have the Spirit. But you, dear friends, by building yourselves up in your most holy faith and praying in the Holy Spirit, keep yourselves in God's love as you wait for the mercy of our Lord Jesus Christ to bring you to eternal life.* – Jude 1:19-21

6. *Let the message of Christ dwell among you richly as you teach and admonish one another with all wisdom through psalms, hymns, and songs from the Spirit, singing to God with gratitude in your hearts.* – Colossians 3:16

7. *Then you will know the truth, and the truth will set you free.* – John 8:32

8. *Therefore, if anyone is in Christ, the new creation has come: The old has gone, the new is here!* – 2 Corinthians 5:17

9. *Set your minds on things above, not on earthly things.* – Colossians 3:2

10. *The mind governed by the flesh is death, but the mind governed by the Spirit is life and peace.* – Romans 8:6

11. *Above all else, guard your heart, for everything you do flows from it.* – Proverbs 4:23

12. *Stand firm then, with the belt of truth buckled around your waist, with the breastplate of righteousness in place, and with your feet fitted with the readiness that comes from the gospel of peace. In addition to all this, take up the shield of faith, with which you can extinguish all the flaming arrows of the evil one.* – Ephesians 6:14-16

13. *If any of you lacks wisdom, you should ask God, who gives generously to all without finding fault, and it will be given to you. But when you ask, you must believe and not doubt, because the one who doubts is like a wave of the sea, blown and tossed by the wind. That person should not expect to receive anything from the Lord.* – James 1:5-7

14. *Finally, brothers and sisters, whatever is true, whatever is noble, whatever is right, whatever is pure, whatever is lovely, whatever is admirable–if anything is excellent or praiseworthy–think about such things.* – Philippians 4:8

15. *Therefore, since we are surrounded by such a great cloud of witnesses, let us throw off everything that hinders and the sin that so easily entangles. And let us run with perseverance the race marked out for us.* – Hebrews 12:1

16. *Do not be anxious about anything, but in every situation, by prayer and petition, with thanksgiving, present your requests to God. And the peace of God, which transcends all understanding, will guard your hearts and your minds in Christ Jesus.* – Philippians 4:6-7

17. *Create in me a clean heart, O God, and renew a steadfast spirit within me.* – Psalm 51:10

18. *Yet those who wait for the LORD Will gain new strength; They will mount up with wings like eagles, They will run and not get tired, They will walk and not become weary.* – Isaiah 40:31

19. *Therefore we do not lose heart, but though our outer man is decaying, yet our inner man is being renewed day by day.* – 2 Corinthians 4:16

20. *You were taught, with regard to your former way of life, to put off your old self, which is being corrupted*

by its deceitful desires; to be made new in the attitude of your minds; and to put on the new self, created to be like God in true righteousness and holiness.
– Ephesians 4:22-24

BIBLIOGRAPHY

"Free." *Merriam-Webster.com Dictionary*, Merriam-Webster, https://www.merriamwebster.com/dictionary/free. Accessed 9 Nov. 2020.

New King James Version Study Bible. Nashville, Tennessee: Thomas Nelson Publishers, 2007.

"20 Inspirational Bible Verses about Renewing Your Mind." *Smart and Relentless*, http://smartandrelentless.com/7922-2/. Accessed 9 Nov. 2020.

www.ingramcontent.com/pod-product-compliance
Lightning Source LLC
Chambersburg PA
CBHW051854160426
43209CB00006B/1298